Longshoreman

Longshoreman

by

Benjamin Pond

JANUS PUBLISHING COMPANY
London, England

First published in Great Britain 2009
by Janus Publishing Company Ltd,
105-107 Gloucester Place,
London W1U 6BY

www.januspublishing.co.uk

British Library Cataloguing-in-Publication Data
A catalogue record for this book is available from the British Library

ISBN 978-1-85756-664-2

Cover Design: Janus Publishing Company
Cover photograph: Ben Pond
Image supplied by Michael Pond

Printed in Great Britain by the MPG Books Group, Bodmin and King's Lynn

Contents

1

Garden by the River

As I stood looking across the water at my old home, I began to realise that if there was an answer to everything, that if we really knew everything, how drab and dreary this world would be. Angling, perhaps more than anything else, makes us aware of how true these facts actually are. Anglers never do solve all the problems of either sea or river and thus it is that angling becomes the greatest of all sports and pursuits, if only because it is so closely aligned with nature.

Yes, across the water stands a large, old house with its garden alongside the little River Anton. The old summer house has collapsed and lies hidden under a huge mass of ivy; the same ivy that once threatened to engulf it in 1902 had at last succeeded. Some fifty-eight years have elapsed since I left the ancient town of Andover, the scene of my childhood. I now stand and gaze at what was once my home, the garden my playground, the river my delight. Yes, the little river that had destined my future, my very life, a life perhaps unique.

I stay for perhaps twenty minutes, looking at the old scene, and then move away filled with emotion; a car nearly bowls me over, so I sit down on a wayside seat. I think back to those early days when, with a ball of string and eel hooks, I killed many a 2 lb trout.

But there are no longer any big trout there today, perhaps pollution is the reason for that, or maybe it was because the water was sometimes dammed upstream for repairs to the mill wheel. By the time the water below the mill had almost drained away for an hour or more, the natives would come along with baskets and collect the fish; I am sure that I was not the only guilty one. Elephants from the circus would be brought to the river, where they would lie down and squirt water over the spectators – this was much enjoyed by the elephants, if no one else.

I think back to when I was six years old and my sister was four – to a day when we picked all the apples and threw them into the river, just to see the town urchins up to their necks in water, grabbing the fruit. It was no Garden of Eden for us when our parents found the orchard bare.

At about that time, I wanted better tackle, but my tuppence a week was going on ice creams, which were a new thing then, so to raise capital, I began to sell horse manure at a penny a bucket. Soon, I was able to buy a rod, 3s 6d, and a reel for 2s 6d, and by this time I had become a determined angler. Also with bucket and shovel, I kept the surrounds of the town hall tidy, which was all to the good, my father being mayor at the time.

In those days, there was no keeping up with the Joneses and my father, being a liberal kind of man, gave away a fortune to the poor of the town. He also provided the site for the new Methodist Chapel (half of our riverside garden) and this greatly curtailed my angling activity, so I became a poacher on the nearby River Test.

At the great age of seven, I could read tolerably well, so for an outlay of tuppence per week, I began to take the "green 'un" as the *Fishing Gazette* was called, which I continued to buy for the next sixty years. My first readings of this paper filled me with enthusiasm; it told me of species I'd never even dreamed about. It told me how to catch many big fish and I discovered that the local streams such as the Test and Anton were not the only two "fishy" rivers, and that there were sea fish waiting, open-mouthed, to be caught all round the British Isles.

Let me say that this story, covering sixty years of events, adventure and unique experiences, is being recorded in consecutive order – I may have to refer back here and there, but only if or where necessary.

Going back to those early days, it came to my attention that there was a very large trout, over 4 lb, on private water that lay beneath a willow bough. Several gentlemen had tried to entice this fish with a variety of flies, but had failed to tempt it, so, taking my sister, at dusk I decided that this fish must be caught. Soon, we saw it, a worm was cast and by chance, it dropped right in front of this monster – it took the worm and the fun began. A long-lasting battle ensued. I had no net, and when I did eventually get both hands upon my prize it was quite dark. In fact, it was so dark that we were both afraid to venture into the dense woods where the path led to our house, so we crawled into a fowl-house nearby and must have fallen asleep.

What a commotion was going on in Andover, of which we, of course, knew nothing; our parents must have thought us to be drowned. At about 2 a.m., we were both awakened by voices and the glare of a carriage lamp; a policeman and the gent who owned this fishery were peering through the doorway.

'Gracious,' the gent muttered, 'they've got one of my fish. Why, it's the big one we can't catch. Arrest 'em, policeman.'

'But they be too young, 'sides, what's a fish matter?' was the reply.

The gent picked up the trout, with about a pound of fowl droppings adhering to it, before relenting, saying, 'Must be over 5 lb, but let the kids keep it; after all, perhaps 'tis best out of the water, we were becoming almost demented with frustration.'

So we were taken home and put to bed.

That same year, the first double-decker bus ever to be seen outside London was put into service in Andover; it was much higher than those of today and had an open top. But no one would ride in or upon it, as they all said it would be sure to topple over. At night, when it returned to the market, it had to negotiate a sharp bend and half the town would assemble, expecting to see it overturn. I think it went back to the city in the end.

Then there was the day when I took my two young cousins and four other boys to Clatford, two miles downriver, where we found a boat, all got in and pushed off. We capsized in deep water; how we got out I can't recall, but on a recount there were still seven of us in the gang. Despite my correct estimate, the police and the boat owner searched the river and a rod I had hidden in a bush was found and confiscated, so there was good reason to mourn for one absent friend.

It now seemed that my parents were a bit concerned about me. They called in Dr Barnes; he tapped every inch of my cranium, producing a sound like that of a kettledrum.

He said to my mother, 'Don't worry too much about the lad, things may become alright, can't find anything. In fact, I can't find anything there at all.'

As this story unfolds, you may think that the old doctor had surmised correctly. I remember escaping through a side door and regaining the river.

As time went on, trout were becoming scarcer and scarcer and my catches lighter and lighter; the two cats grew thinner and thinner, and at the age of eight I was becoming "unemployed". But if the trout are slow on the old uptake on some occasions, it is just as well – there will be some fish left for me to look after in days to come. However, a miracle was soon to happen; a new "situation" was to be found for me.

2

Villa by the Sea

Most of us have done a few silly things at one time or another and it so happens that I seem to have done far more than the average person. Mind, I was always slow to grasp things, backwards at school and never fitted in with town life. To gaze into shop windows, to walk up one street and down the next street, never appealed. There was no desire to rise in the social class, sea level suited me best.

Had I taken over my father's drapery business, I could have been a wealthy man. The concern is worth a six-figure sum today, but to spend a lifetime behind a counter selling reels of cotton was not my intention, so now I am living a lowly life, far more content and happier than many a rich man.

Here, I digress back to 1905, when my father bought a villa down in Bournemouth. We moved by rail – family, furniture and two lean cats, the trout having become few and far between. On the evening of the day we arrived, my mother took me to the cliff top to see the sea for the first time. I was spellbound. I gazed at the vast expanse of water, at the distant horizon, where did it end?

At last, my mother said, 'Come along, there's a lot more must be unpacked.' Then she dragged me back inland.

I slept little that night, perhaps because of some loose fish hooks in my bed. But early I rose, evaded the household and reached the square. Arriving outside Toogood's shellfish shop, I bought tuppence worth of cockles, dashed through the lower gardens and on to the pier, where I lowered my line, but it would not sink. So I found a paperweight on some steamer bills and dropped my line to the bottom, but still no bites. I noticed that paper bills were coming down like a snowstorm, and it was then that I learned what the meaning of "putting the fish down" really meant.

But one fish made a mistake and at the end of three hours, I landed a whiting, unaided, all of 3 oz. I was so elated with my catch that I dashed off home, arriving just after the fishmonger had departed. Nobody showed the slightest interest in my whiting, except the two cats, who finally shared it.

The first visit to that pier was to be followed by many hundreds. I had begun a life of a thousand diversions that were to be either directly or indirectly connected with angling, plus some adventures of a very "fishy" nature.

Over 19,000 days of angling were to account for over 1,390,000 fish, both sea and river. This may seem a huge total, but one has to think back to the days when we caught between 150 and 300 mixed fish at sea, and an average of 80 from the river – we shall see later how this was accomplished on a crude and a limited range of tackle. Knowledge of our sport was not derived from books; it was all learned the hard way. The best way, if you could spare the time, was by being "on the spot", by experimenting.

One must recall that sixty years ago, the sea was a clean place – no deposits of oil or millions of particles of rubber from cars going down the drains and into the sea, or tar from the roads and other poisonous matter, and nor was there much inshore trawling at that time.

I take this extract from *Angler's World* (September 1962), which I wrote when referring to 1908:

> ... thousands of fish stayed round the pier piles at Bournemouth for months on end, any daft angler could fill a sack, any day. I was as daft as the rest of 'em. I played truant. Friday afternoons was Latin. How I hated it, never got beyond the first two of the five declensions, Mensa and Domino – I'd nearly forgotten it. Nine out of eleven Friday afternoons that term I was absent, gone fishin.
>
> I knew that my form master thought I was mad; he followed me to the pier one day to see what strange rites were performed.
>
> At the end of that day he was more than mildly off his rocker; yes, it was me teaching him. He came on the Saturday with a shilling hand-line and twopenny worth of cockles. He landed a plaice of nearly 4 lb. Me – well, it was just one of those off days ...

But I was learning all the time, even if not at school.

I got to know the "regulars" and visitors on the pier. There was one fellow, Old Moore, his name was really Moore, and I got to know him more and more. He possessed a prominent proboscis, which was highly coloured due to frequent visits to the Pier Hotel. It is said that one night, when the pier-head light failed, the pier-master bribed Old Moore to stand there all night, and thus a possible shipwreck was prevented by a "shipwreck".

One night, I stayed on the lower deck and fished until it was getting very late, catching some pollack around 2 lb apiece, while the Municipal Orchestra on the upper deck played pleasant refrains. A gent whom I knew came down the iron stairway. It was the borough coroner and he said, 'You should be in bed by now.'

'What,' I retorted, 'when fish are on the feed? Besides, it's cost me tuppence to get on here.'

Relenting somewhat at my abrupt reply, I presented him with a brace (pure purist talk) of pollack, whereupon he gave me a half-sovereign (it was 1908) saying, 'Get yourself a pier season ticket in the morning.'

So I duly arrived at the pier entrance soon after four o'clock the next morning, waiting only four hours for the first official to come along. I was the first customer and I went on and off all day long, until finally they locked me out for the night, after having twice oiled the turnstiles. I passed through sixty-six times in all, which was how the term "clicketty-click" came into use, and that became my title as the turnstiles continued to click away.

What with dumping a pound of lead upon the copper dome of the bandstand during that Rubenstein's delightful *Melody in F,* also decorating most of the seats with split lugworms and ripe cockles, and wearing out those turnstiles, I was none too popular with the pier staff.

Let us stay awhile upon the pier. A year has passed 'tis true, but where else should I be, but looking into the sea? A competition is about to begin, I pay a shilling and enter, and then I draw a number out of a hat – it is number twenty-seven. My peg is just behind the surf, top deck, a likely spot. Haynes and the "Irishman" draw the lower deck – they will both use live prawns, just right for some pollack. The three dabs I caught earlier I wrapped up in paper and put in an inside pocket.

The pier bell rings, eighty-three lines go into the sea, everyone is keyed up. For a time, we wait hopefully and put up with the visitors who get in our way and ask silly questions, tapping their foreheads as they get silly answers, and walk away.

I catch a small bass and my trembling hands unhook it and place it safely in my creel. Others, either side of me, get a fish. I get another bass, then a flounder, then three more bass, and then the bell rings and we all gather at the bandstand. Here, the mayor has to present the prizes. What a crowd – eighty-three anglers, the officials and about 600 spectators.

The mayor reads out the list of prizewinners. I come third, but there is an error, my name was read out as being fifth. Did I have the nerve to go up to his worship, before the entire audience, and make a protest? No, not me. Haines and the "Irishman" easily got the first two awards. The chap who took my prize received a whacking-great roach basket, one of those things one sits on – or in; we call them lumber rooms down South. Now Old Moore had one of these, he used it to hawk watercress around to get money for beer. I already had a French creel. What a good job I had not protested – fifth prize was a lovely leather tackle case with nine compartments.

As soon as I got it, away I fled, before they might discover their mistake. I was hot with perspiration – what an ordeal! Those three little dabs in my inner pocket were almost done to a turn – no wonder angling is the greatest pastime in the world. Far more exciting and rewarding than watching the Cup Final, holing in one, shooting a stag or getting the Freedom of the Borough.

3

Missing Pennies

The year following, my season pier ticket having expired, I had to produce tuppence to go through the turnstiles each day, and I went on most days. This was becoming rather expensive, so I decided to do what I saw other boys do, which was to climb among the iron girders beneath the deck and so reach the steamer landing stage at the far end. In performing the necessary acrobatics, my tuppence slipped out of my pocket and into the sea. "Out of pocket" expenses it certainly was.

At about this time, I was becoming exceedingly fond of ships and was often taking trips on the paddle steamers. One very hot day I caught the *Balmoral* to Swanage, spent a lot on lemonade, and then discovered that I was one penny short for my pier toll to board the boat, for which I had a return ticket. I was desperate. I walked up and down Institute Road a dozen times, what could I do? Then, just before the last boat was due to leave, I saw a man who I recalled as being a traveller and who called monthly at my father's shop in Andover. Nervously, I approached him and explained my plight. Would he lend me just one penny? I stammered out. He gave me a florin. 'Forget about it,' he said, when I told him he would be repaid.

And he was – my father gave him a big order on his next visit to the shop.

I became fond of Swanage; there was never another place like it. Sections of its foreshore consist of rock, sandstone, pebbles, shingle, chalk, clay and a long stretch of golden sand. I had a fishing mate at that time, Alan Mugford, who has long since gone to Australia. He was about my age, ten and a bit, and one day he suggested a night's fishing on Swanage Pier. So, the next evening, we caught the last boat at Bournemouth for this Dorset resort.

Upon landing, we went inland to wait for the pier staff to leave for home. As soon as the staff had gone, we returned to the pier, climbed over the locked gate and made for the port-side landing stage. Here, we found a gas jet light, only used when a late steamer was berthed. This light shone seawards, so we pulled the chain and on came the light, just what we wanted.

That night, we caught pollack, smelts and wrasse and, to crown it all, Muggy, as I shall refer to him, got a conger of about 16 lb and I pulled in a bass of around 10 lb. By about 4 a.m., the fish ceased to feed, so we went to the top deck and put a penny in a slot machine. Out came a packet containing two cigarettes, the ideal opportunity to indulge in a first smoke, or so we thought. But no – the tobacco was soaking wet, either from sea spray or damp air. Cigarettes, two big ones for a penny, ye gods.

We started for home at six o'clock, each of us carrying about 27 lb of fish, besides the tackle. Our route to the ferry at the mouth of Poole Harbour lay over the Purbeck hills, 700 feet high. Crossing over, we had a further seven miles to walk, making fourteen miles in all. Muggy was carrying his conger over his shoulder and as we neared Bournemouth, a dark-skinned gentleman followed behind, muttering, 'Dats a beeg snake, dat is'. It was noon when we reached our homes, fagged out; how we did this long walk I can't fully remember.

I little knew that later in life I was to sail into Swanage Bay hundreds of times; nor of the hazards that were to befall me.

To sail on: as a boy, I found Bournemouth Pier much to my liking. There were plenty of fish in great variety, the sea was free from contamination before Man had found the use of oil and detergents, you could drink the salt water – I did, half a pint most days – the sea never got any lower, I got quite a lot higher, and I also taught myself to swim, drinking a lot more seawater whilst learning.

I suppose that I chose Muggy because he was an untidy little lad like me – carefree, with uncombed hair, always game for a bit of fishing or a twenty-mile walk. His father owned the local gymnasium, so we were both "put through the ropes" by Mr Geoff Mugford.

At this early age, I had already decided that I would not become a slave to convention. No hooter was ever going to tell me to go home from some morbid, indoor employment, and nor would I take over my father's shop – me, selling reels of cotton behind a counter? Never. Town life was not for me, I was to avoid wearing collars and ties, and I was to go barefoot summer and winter, to even live by barter.

Although I can probably tie almost every known type of nautical knot – and some alleged knots that aren't knots – I am unable to tie the simple knot that one does with collar and tie. In fact, I have never even attempted to tie such a knot; I always found it much quicker and far easier to use a clip-on bow. Why ever town chaps fiddle about with collars and ties I don't know. What a waste of time, how half-strangled they must feel and how early in life they seem to go bald and have to wear spectacles. What "spectacles" they look, too. I have noticed the city type in particular, who favour stiff collars; they soon become bald and can't see anything clearly. Wearing a fisherman's jersey, of course, makes a collar superfluous. Only on the rare occasions that I took fish to my sister did I dig out a soft collar and bow. I can even remember the day when I had taken a four-pound plaice to her and was returning down Poole high street, yes, with collar and bow.

Prestige and conformity meant less than nowt. How I pitied the city man who was –

"Each day pulled up to London town by train, and each night pulled back down again."

We youngsters could walk in those days. What about that morning when another pal Reg Gladney woke me up at 5.00 a.m. – would lads of today do this sort of thing?

I must have been about eleven years of age when I implored my father that I needed a boat. At last, he assented and I bought a twenty-foot sailing boat with two masts and four sails at Christchurch. The owner let me have it for £9, as his wife and daughter were afraid to go out in it on the open sea.

The morning came when I had a fair wind and tide to sail her round to Poole, some eighteen miles away. Now I had never hoisted a sail before, so, with so many dangling ropes suspended from the two masts, I just did not know which was which and what was what. Already, a large number of spectators had assembled on the quay to wish me bon voyage or something like it. But with an audience, I just did not have the nerve to raise a single sail, so I rowed the two miles to the harbour mouth.

How I got up the mainsail and one jib, I'll never know, but I made good progress and was off Bournemouth Pier at 2.15 p.m., where I had promised to pick up Muggy at 2.30 p.m. He was there waiting. Soon, the wind fell light, but we managed to enter Poole Harbour on the turn of the tide, at 5.30 p.m.

Leaving the boat for the night, we tied her to a heavy stone with only a seven-foot length of rope; we had not allowed for the tide to rise seven feet or more, so the next morning when we arrived, there was no boat. Upon gazing across the western part of the harbour, we could see our precious craft aground on Stony Island. By the time had we hired a boat and towed our own one back against wind and tide, half the day was gone. Yes, I've learned the hard way often enough, but, believe me, it's the best way. I've never regretted having done so.

Within a fortnight, I had mastered this craft, could run up all four sails and go out in really rough weather conditions, but I had a few narrow squeaks and anxious moments in the process. From this boat, I caught many bass in the East Looe Channel, and away farther at sea I got a variety of fish, including mackerel and bream – never a dull moment. It was then that I knew the life I was meant to lead, sometimes afloat or otherwise along the shores at the riverside.

But, as yet, there was much to learn about the "fishy" family and the lures to catch them. Then there was the art of beachcombing, the risky game of smuggling, weathering a gale at night and existing without money. All this was to come.

4

Inland is the River

Two miles from my new home I found the River Stour and the village of Throop. I also got to know the local farmer, who also managed the mill and the fishing rights. He was very kind to me and gave me free coarse fishing in return for me doing odd jobs on his farm. I was in clover in more ways than one. I also fished the mill stream, which was free to the lads of the village. We made huge catches by using mill sweepings to get the fish on the feed.

Between this village and my home was another farm, owned by a grumpy old farmer Brown. I used to take a short cut across his fields and he set PC Holmes on my tracks. On three separate occasions, this bobby pulled me out of the field by my ears; I can now sail much faster before the wind.

Muggy came out on his bike one morning to look for me at the river and he caught two ducklings, putting one in each pocket of his coat. Later, we took the narrow lane for home, Muggy pushing the bike. Coming towards us was PC Holmes and as we neared him, those two wretched ducklings started to squeak like mad. All he said was, 'Thic ther' crock could do wiv a drop o' oil.'

Before long, I began to follow the salmon anglers. I was not too lucky at first, but at last they could not cast me off and, after gaffing a few fish and carrying their gear, I was made welcome. Then came the day when a gent said that he would be in London for two weeks and that I could try and catch myself a salmon. I did just that. I saw a fish rise, on the second cast it took, did not play it, too excited, dragged the 17 lb salmon ashore through the sedges and sat on it. You see, my line was 40 lb breaking strain. As the season went on, I had other offers to have odd days and got several salmon, up to 32 lb. Seems I was born lucky: a variety of sea fishing to the south and a wonderful river two miles to the north.

13

On this farm at Throop, I spent many days doing various sorts of jobs for twelve shillings a week. The evenings would be occupied by fishing the river.

I never worked to fixed hours, came and went as I liked. I also became fond of the horses and the first time I took them to the river for a drink, I went head first into the water off the old mare's back. I can also recall the afternoon when I had to put four horses into long ground. I had just released them when a tiny plane tried to make a forced landing, overshot our field and went through the hedge into the next field. Because of the gap it made, I had to catch the excited horses and take them to another field. The pilot was unhurt, but the plane was just a small heap of canvas and plywood, and yet twenty-seven huge army lorries and a staff car came to remove the bits and pieces, knocking down both of our gateposts on entering the field.

Adjoining the farm was the Earl of Malmesbury's estate and among the staff was a lad of poor intellect. One morning, the old Earl met this lad at South Lodge Gate and asked him where he was going.

'To get some lard, me Lard, ther' be no lard in the larder, me Lard,' answered the lad.

After a while, I got tired of farm work (I had done everything except milking and ploughing), and the sea called once more, so I returned to saltwater fishing with a vengeance. Back on the pier, I saw anglers doing the overhead cast. Surely I could do this – or so I thought. In bringing my rod upwards with a mighty swing, my one-pound lump of lead broke away and went sailing up, up, into the clouds. But it also had to come down. It did, bonk on top of the copper dome of the bandstand, just as the Municipal Orchestra was playing that serene number known as *Melody in F.* I even had the nerve to go up among that great audience to recover my lead.

'Don't you ever do that again,' said the pier master, as the band once more began to play – somewhat out of tune, I thought.

What a laugh we had one August Regatta Day; an incident entirely unrehearsed. The mayor and corporation, in top hats and frock coats, had assembled on a large, flat pontoon to watch the rowing, swimming and other marine events. Now all this activity might be interesting enough, you might well think, but it so happened that an

14

angler on the pier hooked a very large mullet – his rod was bent double as he tried to coax his fish to the steps.

Anyway, the noble gentlemen on the pontoon had no more interest in the sports; in fact, they were all watching the angler, moving in one mass to the pontoon's side, causing it to tilt at such a steep angle that the said noble gentlemen and others all slid into the sea. Top hats floated around, two of the councillors managed to swim to the pier, where they were both "landed" by anglers, and others were picked up by some of the yachtsmen. Yes, we laughed our heads off, gave 'em a cheer, too, and another cheer for the angler who landed his 6 lb mullet at the steps, completely oblivious to what was happening nearby – his thoughts were only on landing his prize.

I suppose I had the fishing bug good and proper. I can remember one particular morning when I set off on a two-mile walk to Boscombe Pier at 5.30 a.m. I had got nearly there, when a milkman pulled me up and said, 'Where's yer boots?' I still had my bedroom slippers on. So you see how keen I was in pursuit of fishes. My parents were still concerned about me though; perhaps they had not forgotten old Dr Barnes' remarks. My father would give me a funny look, as I sometimes cursed the wind at the breakfast table. I would be looking out of the window and if I noticed a leaf so much as quiver, I would rave like mad. I well knew what it would be like on an exposed shore two hours later. In one week, two hats had left my head and sailed into the stormy sea, so my father told me to go and buy a real sou'wester. He said, 'Get one two sizes too big.' Failing to see his meaning, I did just that. The very first day I wore it, into the sea it went, so I cursed the wind to anglers both on my left and right as I stood on that windy pier that day.

One very rough night a steamer went aground at Southbourne, three miles east of the pier. It was the Leander, weighing in at 3,800 tons. The crew were saved by coastguards, who hauled them up the cliffs. Captain Kettley was the master at the time. His home was only a mile inland, yet the ship did not normally voyage in these waters. I knew his family; in fact, I went to school with three of his children. The ship remained aground for four months, the family spending much time aboard; eventually, a channel was dredged and the Leander was refloated, little the worse for wear.

Later, there was a very heavy gale and the Treveal went on to Kimmeridge Rocks. The entire crew of thirty-eight lost their lives. My sailing boat broke away that very night. I found her the next day among some gorse bushes, undamaged. That just goes to show how high the seas rose; a gale like that might happen once in a hundred years.

Muggy and I went to fish off a wreck once, where we had a good catch. By the afternoon, the sun was very hot, so we strung the fish up and lowered them into the sea on a line. Nothing else was caught in the next two hours, so we hauled up the line with the fish – or what was left of them; crabs had eaten every bit of flesh, so we only pulled up the bones. We were so disgusted that we went and bought a shilling's worth of stinking whiting from an ancient fisherman, and then went home and said we had caught 'em!

5

On Guard at Herne Bay

Must have been about 1912 when I had a craze to plant horse chestnuts. Today, two magnificent trees stand in their place in Bournemouth. They had sprung from two of the conkers, which I had pushed into the soil all those years back. Often, I go and take a look at my handiwork, perhaps the memories of past days gives me a feeling of contentment.

But to take up my story: as a lad, I began to play golf. I could not afford to pay for a round, so I would go out on the course before the staff were even out of bed. Nor could I afford the golf balls. But this was overcome by going to a pond which was at the side of the tenth green. Numerous balls went into this pond, some floated and others sank according to the amount of elastic in them. Using a long, crooked stick, I would rake the bed of the pond and averaged five balls a visit. I raked in other things as well and sometimes I would put my hand in to pick up the object and it would be a horrible old toad.

I was never at a loss for something to do: I made my own bow and arrows, had an air gun, went on long walks, had books from the library and also had pet animals. I even had fish, which I kept in tanks of rainwater. Every morning, I would immerse my face in this water, keeping my eyes half open for thirty seconds and never had to wear spectacles thanks to doing this; what the fish thought of this daily diversion I don't know.

Time passed quickly, and then came the First World War, at which point I joined the Hampshire's, though under age, and was sent home to Herne Bay.

One morning, an officer called out, 'All men of eighteen years of age fall out, too young to be drafted to France.'

17

Some seven of us came forward; one had a Charlie Chaplin moustache, he was thirty-eight; 'Sorry,' said the officer, 'I've got you down as eighteen, so you can't go.' The chap wasn't sorry.

Each company, to be of uniform size for marching to church, had to consist of 200 men. Those above this number would be dismissed, so there was always a crowd pushing for places at the end of the column to avoid going to church. One Sunday, the captain said to these fellows at the end of the column, 'You are the ones that ought to be converted, I will dismiss the men who are at the other end,' and he did.

Our pay was three shillings per week. Out of this vast wage, we had to buy all our polish and stamps, and we would also have to get haircuts and penny cups of tea at the YMCA. A few months later, our pay was increased to three shillings and sixpence a week. To receive it, three men would be named together and a ten-shilling note and a sixpence would be handed to one of the three chaps. You would then see groups of threes running around to find a shop that would change the note for a share out.

Often, it became my job to do guard duties on the pier, which was nearly three-quarters of a mile in length. At night, I would often have fishing lines out at the far end; seems I was supposed to supply the battalion with fish. Now the pier was mined at the far end, also at the halfway point, just in case the Germans took a fancy to this resort. The mines could be exploded by pressing two buttons in the guardroom at the entrance to the pier. Whoever was on guard would go up with the pier if "it" happened.

One bitterly cold night when I was doing my spell, to keep warm, I marched from end to end of that slippery, frosted deck. Halfway along, down I went, my rifle butt hitting the deck with a thud that must have been heard in faraway Folkestone. I sat there for a whole minute, expecting the pier to go up at any moment. Then I heard the guard turn out, one shouting: 'Press both buttons.' Then another voice chimed in, 'No, wait a minute, he might have some fish.' Seems a few whiting saved my life that night. Wherever I went during those war years there was always a fishing line in my kitbag, which I used at Plymouth, Clacton, Deben Estuary and Felixstowe.

The only benefit for me of being in the army was to learn Morse at a brigade signalling school and to learn how to ride a bike. But I hated this life – too much routine and red tape. I was granted my first leave after eleven months: five days; three days at home and two days travelling to and fro. No, army life did not agree with me; too used to my early years of freedom.

I will pass over most of those war years. I did nothing heroic, but spent the last seven weeks in hospital back at Felixstowe, where I could see the sea from my window. As I lay in bed, I saw the entire fleet of German submarines being escorted into Harwich. They were spaced about a quarter of a mile apart and they took two days in all in arriving. As I lay there, I thought about the things which I had hidden down rabbit burrows before I had joined up three years back. Were they still there? Rods, reels, sandshoes and bait boxes had all been stowed underground amid the sand dunes on a wild and lonely shore at Poole Harbour. How I longed to get back to my old haunts. Soon, I was to be well again and free, yes, free.

In January 1919, I left hospital and got my discharge a week later, arriving home one morning at 2.50 a.m. But my family were both surprised and delighted at the wanderer's return, as I had not written to say that I was going to be discharged.

Now being able to ride a bike, thanks to the army, I borrowed my sister's and a few days later I was off to Shell Bay, which is on the south end of Poole Harbour. Sure enough, all the gear in the rabbit burrows was intact and in reasonably good order.

Ah, Shell Bay and Studland Heath, which I had got to know so well before the war. This great heath stretching nearly ten miles in one direction and six miles another, is interspersed with forest, copse, lakes and the haunted house – but we'll come to that later. The wild harbour coastline is much indented, with long creeks running into the undulating heathland, and no roads or habitations for miles.

Of course, today it is overrun by thousands of day trippers; a floating bridge carries both them and their cars from Sandbanks over to Shell Bay. From here, a new road runs for four miles over the heath to Studland, but you will learn of the glorious years which I have spent in or around this delightful coastal area of south-east Dorset. But before I tell of those glorious years to be, I was destined to spend a few months in Alvediston in South Wiltshire, far from the haunts I knew so well.

On second thoughts, this chapter seems to be too short, so before I begin about Alvediston – nice word, ain't it; sounds like "'alf the distance" – I will tell any young, single readers amongst you just how to hoodwink nosy parkers should you take the plunge and get married. You will, from time to time, hear about Muggy, but here is what he told me when he got married: he and his wife set off from the reception in their car with two fishing rods, leaving their gaping spectators behind, and rode away into the unknown. Reaching a copse, they entered and removed every (?) particle of confetti. Yes, you see, there is a way of concealing that you have only just got married when you meet the other guests at your hotel. And it works, no matter if you are an angler or not, provided you both carry a fishing rod. (If you are not an angler, this may well help you to become one; also, it will be an excuse for you to go out and see the boys.)

Now this is what you must do upon arriving at the hotel: walk boldly across the lawn, each carrying a rod – not hand in hand, mind. Funny thing was though, it failed to work in Muggy's case. Most of the guests were seated in the loggia, so, on entering, Muggy, with a most gracious bow and magnificent sweeping gesture, removed his trilby and 417 bits of confetti came flying out from the upturned brim onto the heads of the assembled company. Embarrassing? As to whether it was 417 particles of coloured little bits of paper I do not know, even if it was only seven it was still seven too many.

There was one other trick they intended to play, which was to drop bits of nylon (I mean fishing line, not clothing) on the stairs when shown to their rooms; this idea had now become superfluous. Bit fishy, wasn't it?

6

Overturned Wagon

At the end of the First World War, there were about 3 million unemployed. I was among them, with no hope of getting a job.

My father had just retired at that time and had bought a farmhouse at Alvediston in South Wiltshire, and he suggested that I left our house in Bournemouth and came up to him for a few weeks to help him to get the garden into good shape, also to make up bundles of sticks for firewood in the nearby woods. This I did, much to his satisfaction. Then, bidding farewell, I set out for Belchalwell, a rather isolated hamlet in the centre of Dorset, lying at the foot of Bulbarrow Hill, 909 feet above sea level.

I had heard that they needed someone to remove moss from the hillside, which was to be taken to the nearest station. This moss is hand-picked and tied in bunches, 144 to the sack, and is sent to Covent Garden. My job was to load the sacks on to the wagon. Then, leading the horse, I would slowly retreat down the steep, chalky down by way of what is called a "sideline" track. The drug is fixed under the inner back wheel and in particularly bad spots, one has to chain the offside back wheel, thus locking both back wheels. Incidentally, the drug is also known as the drag shoe. Once off the great hill, I would take my load to Shillingstone Station, enter the weighbridge and then put the sacks of moss in the covered goods van.

One morning, I had an extra high load and it had been raining, so the sacks were heavier than usual. Reaching a very bad bit of the track, over went the wagon, the ropes snapped and my forty-eight sacks went rolling down the hill for half a mile, bowling over some cows, which put their heads down to them. Finding the boss, he said, 'I'll show you how to do it next time.'

So the next morning, he led the horse and I followed behind the load, which was again heavy because of the falling rain. Reaching the spot where I had upset my load, over it went once more. Laugh! I couldn't stop! Down the hill went the sacks, ever gaining momentum; one crashed through the fence of my boss' back garden, going straight into his greenhouse, also bringing down a line of washing. I tendered my resignation before he could give me the sack for my outburst of frivolity. I'd had enough. Luckily, the horse was alright, even after the two upsets.

There were no other jobs in this area, so I began a dried fish round to all the mid-Dorset villages on my carrier cycle. My best customers were the gypsies on top of Bulbarrow Down. Returning from a round one evening, I needed to come back over the hill in order to leave eighteen pairs of kippers at the camp. Pushing my bike up the steep slope for nearly two miles, I came to the three blazing fires. Around each fire was a ring of merry people, each holding a roasted pheasant and doing their best to spoil the look of it. I was asked to join them and was given a bird, as two of them were "men of the road", who had gatecrashed the feasters. Everyone received a half-cup of brandy to finish off. I passed over a newspaper to old Ma Cooper, Queen of the Tribe.

'Can't read very well, none o' us bin learned,' she said.

So, by the light of the fire, I read off just the headlines: "Robbery with violence", "Murder charge against youth", "Attack on landlord", "Child killed by car", "Raid on bank" being just some of the headings they all listened to as I read.

For a few moments, no one spoke, and then an old fellow remarked, 'Good job us be away from all o' they sort, us do know how to live an' mind our own bizness.'

On those three fires I reckoned they must have roasted no less than thirty-six pheasants. But how had they obtained so many plump birds? I found the answer about a year later. I was reading a South-Dorset paper, when I came to a short paragraph about poaching:

BRANDY GETS THE BIRDS
Again reports have come to light of pheasants being found in a stupefied condition and unable to get off the ground. It is thought that poachers, knowing that the birds are to

be located near to blackberry bushes, must have placed some of these berries on the ground, which had been soaked in spirits, possibly brandy.

Thinking back to that night on Bulbarrow, I recalled that my treble tot of brandy contained a blackberry – seems to "add up".

But where was I? Oh, winter was coming on, so I left this part of Dorset and returned to Alvediston to spend a few months in the nearby woods cutting fencing posts and bundles of sticks for firewood. I became interested in the carriers, who made weekly journeys to town. Back in those days, there were no buses and you had to travel with the carrier to get necessities, or ask him to bring back what you required. One of these men was a Mr Peckham of Donhead. He would come through our village, picking up one or more persons here and there on his sixteen-mile trek to the market town. There was no hurry. The horse went at its own rate of speed, taking three hours to get there. Time was of no consequence back then. If we met a postman or the bobby, we had to stop for a long yarn.

By the time we had passed through a chain of villages, the old van would be packed with humanity, and the tail-board and roof with eggs, butter, vegetables and whatnot. If we came to a steep hill, it was "everybody out", and we all had to push from behind. Should anyone miss the carrier en route, it meant waiting a whole week before he came round again. These days, we grumble if we have to wait five minutes for a bus, or if the traffic lights are on red.

How these old carriers managed to remember all they had to do is remarkable, as along the dusty road which passed through the villages, women would stop him on his way. He would be asked to bring back all kinds of things, perhaps a basin, 'but it must fit my kitchen sink and match my wallpaper and not be chipped' – such were the demands.

I recall one return journey when we were packed in like sardines and it was pitch dark, because the rear doors had been closed to keep out the wind and the rain. A parson in the corner had just finished a short sermon to an unseen audience, when a voice muttered, 'Wer' think us be got to now?'

The parson quipped, 'Should think it must be the black hole of Calcutta.'

Then another joined in, 'Ther' baint no sich place as calcutter on thic yer road.'

Then there was the day when a young fellow was asked by a neighbour to bring back a pram on the van. Somehow, he got left behind, so he had to push the pram four miles through the valley. As he passed various cottages, women would call out, 'Be it a boy or a girl?'; 'What be she expectin'?' By the time the poor chap got back, his face was as red as a beetroot, though not from walking.

A funny thing happened when farmer Coombs moved to another farm. When clearing out old straw from the end of a barn, he found an old three-burner oil stove. I'll clean it up and take it to market, he thought. Needn't tell the ole 'oman, mean a few drinks fer I. So he took the stove on his wagon and got twenty-five shillings for it.

Two weeks later, Mrs Coombs had to go to town with the carrier. When she came back, she called out to her husband, 'Come and lend us a 'and. See what a luvly bargin I got ... ony fouwer pun ten.'

Yes, you've guessed it; it was the old stove come back. If ever old farmer Coombs badly needed a drink it was then.

7

Into the Unknown

I had been inland too long and the urge to get back to the coast was too strong, so I resolved to leave Alvediston and go and seek my fortune.

So, on a beautiful June morning in 1921, I loaded up the fore and aft carriers of the old bike with frying pan, kettle, teapot, blanket and many other oddities, and then bade my father farewell and began a 40-mile ride with ten and sixpence in my pocket. My road – if you could call it such – led over the Cranborne Chase, 870 feet high, followed by a trek along a four-mile rutted cart track down into Sixpenny Handley. By the time I came to a small inn at about the halfway point, it was time for a rest and a meal.

I obtained the following:

Bread and cheese	1½ d
Half a pint of ale	1½ d
Bar chocolate	½ d
5 cigarettes	1 d
Box matches	½ d
Newspaper	½ d
Total	**5½ d**

So I had a halfpenny change out of my sixpence. This, I lost playing shove-ha'penny.

A yokel was in the bar with a fishing rod, so I enquired what sport he had had.

'Can't fish, they've just put a new oak rail on the bridge and sap in the wood attracts wasps, might get stung,' he replied.

'Come outside,' I said to the startled piscator as I grabbed his rod, 'I'll show you.'

Reaching the road bridge, I stunned two wasps with the newspaper and using them as bait, immediately caught two trout, and then threw the rod into the astonished hands of the said piscator and departed on my way.

At about 4.45 p.m., I reached Corfe Castle where the great heath began, the heath I loved so much. Some great urge had brought me thus far. I knew not where my bed would be, nor how I would obtain a living, as so many were still unemployed. After a further six miles of crossing over the heath, I came to the fringe of Poole Harbour. Here, in a dell amidst the heather, I unpacked most of my things and then collected fir cones from a nearby group of trees ready for a fire. Next, I went to Redhorn Rocks, managed to find a few ragworm and started fishing with the hand line I had brought along. Soon, I caught two nice flounders. Have you ever tried fine-filleted flounders fried over a fir cone fire? It's fabulous. From the spring at Brand's Ford, I then filled my kettle with enough for four cups of tea. Then, too tired for anything else, I lay down in the heather and slept through the night, regardless of snakes, ants, rats, rabbits or stray cattle treading on me.

When morning came, I ate the second flounder and made tea again. What was I to do? I had "arrived", but what lay before me? Meditating, I decided to leave my "camp" just as it was and cross to the ferry on old Scott's motor boat and go and see Stephens, a boat builder at Sandbanks. I had known him previously; perhaps he might give me a job. He agreed, but he could only give me four days a week at nine pence an hour. I agreed; beggars can't be choosers.

I still had my ten shillings. So, with half of this, I bought bread, butter and other things (owed Scotty for return journey on the ferry), and returned to my night's residence. But how and where could I find lodgings? Then I recalled a lonely hamlet near the shores of Poole Harbour, about two miles away. But no one there had ever heard of taking in a lodger, so, very disappointed, I started to walk away. Then a voice called me back; a man who had once been foreman of what had once been the local clay company had just arrived and had been told I wanted lodgings.

Turning, he said, 'There's two empty cottages, one and six a week rent. They got three rooms each.'

I paid two week's rent there and then, what did it matter if I didn't have a stick of furniture? Although I had the key, I could not face sleeping there in an empty room, what would people think? So it was another night on the heath, followed by a day working at my new job.

Upon telling Stephens how I was situated, he very kindly offered me a chair, some crates, a bucket and other odd articles, saying, 'Take a boat and row across the harbour with the stuff. Matter of fact, you can hang on to that craft, might be handy for a bit of fishing, odd times.'

With a fair tide, I rowed the four miles across the harbour to the south-western shore, unloaded my cargo, and then made several journeys through the woods to my new home with my new possessions. Thus, bit by bit, I fitted out my new home. Being in the woods meant that there was plenty of firewood, and there was also a spring giving a continuous supply of water. But what a strange community I had come into. Of the forty-seven inhabitants, few could read or write. They did not depend on the outside world, they had all they wanted right here: butter, milk, bacon, eggs, vegetables; they even made wine – just half a pint would knock you flat. Soon, I was able to catch plenty of fish and I was able to supply everyone with fish, winkles, picture papers and odd timber I found on the shores. In return, I was given all the kinds of food I required, including bread, which they baked twice a week. No money passed between us, we lived by barter. This was the perfect life, fresh air, good food, work when I liked, with fishing or beachcombing much of the time. By way of a change, I would sometimes do odd gardening jobs at Sandbanks. Thus, I earned extra money to help pay for my new boat.

Walking round Studland Bay one evening, I found a quantity of timber washed ashore after four days of south-easterly winds. The next morning, I borrowed a bigger boat from Mr Stephens and went and fetched this flotsam: planks, pieces of mahogany, blocks of good timber, mops, brooms and deckchairs. He gave me £2 for some of the things, saying, 'Spend it on having a week's holiday.'

But this kind of life was all one long holiday to me and as to how I could possibly spend all this money, all £2 of it, left me puzzled.

Mr Stephens suggested, 'You can have my sailing boat, go to the Isle of Wight.'

So I did. I sailed right round the island and covered 116 miles in six days. I bought food at several resorts and slept in the boat by night, spending two nights and one day at Cowes, due to a dead calm.

Sailing is a tonic to the brain. One becomes quick in thought and action; otherwise, you would either capsize or get a biff on the head as the boom swung inboard on every tack.

8

Lump of Oak

The time had come for Stephens to think about building my boat, a Norge type double-ender, length twenty feet, both ends quarter decked, fishtail rudder. I designed her myself, giving the sides a good rake for buoyancy. Each stem end was to be of oak, 120 degrees. At first, Stephens could not make sense of my crude drawings and nor could he make much progress, having only one oak stem. Now it is exceedingly hard to get pieces of angle oak to exact measurements, due to their natural bend, so I hunted around for miles, but no luck. Then at last I heard that old Jim Coffin, a fisherman, had a stock of oak at the back of the Ship Inn, Swanage. Sure enough, he had the very piece, about 70 lb in its rough state.

'What's want for it?' I asked, ready to pay a sovereign.

'Four bob to you, mate, seeing it be fer yer new boat. Come on in, let's celebrate the occasion.'

So into the Ship Inn we went. There were five more fishermen there and all of them wanted to hear what the oak was for. Old Jim treated the assembled company four times round, and then we went out to secure the lump of oak on to the frame of my bike. This took about half a mile of cord; as to where it came from, I was past caring. Eventually, I set off, pushing my load, but when I got to Institute Road, I kept finding myself on the wrong side of the road.

Reaching Station Road corner, a stout police sergeant stopped me and said, 'Go and lie down on the sands with the donkeys.'

I must have slept until about 5.30 p.m. Four pints was too much for me ...

Near my cottage was a large plantation of chestnut trees. We'd had a very rough October and the nuts lay thick on the ground, so I began to pick them up and sold quantities of them in Bournemouth, Poole,

29

Parkstone and Swanage. I handled almost one and a half tons in all, getting fourpence a pound at first, before dropping to tuppence. The Spanish and French nuts were late coming over, so I could find a ready market anywhere.

Back in those days, there were no more than a dozen private houses in Sandbanks, eight coastguards' cottages, and the Haven Inn. Huge sand dunes, partly covered in marram grass, extended over much of the area and the sea bordered three sides.

I became friendly with an Irish lady who gave me all sorts of jobs, painting, gardening, rustic work and the like. She kindly offered me the use of a hut, which was in a sandy hollow about seventy yards or more from her house. I fitted this out with a bed, an oil stove, a cupboard which served as a table, and a box as a seat. This hut proved to be a most useful asset, as I could sleep here if the tide was adverse or if it blew a gale, so I did not always go back to the hamlet at night. I could also keep spare clothes, fishing gear and tools to hand.

The roof was boarded and tarred, and the four sides were made of trellis covered in hessian, yet with my stove, it was warm enough inside, even in winter. What a labour-saving abode it proved to be. Without rising from my box seat, I could prepare a meal from the cupboard, light the stove, make tea, put things back in the cupboard, put out the stove and then slosh tea leaves out of the small open window onto the sand below. On one side, piled high against the hut, was a huge nest of wood ants, but they never intruded; may have been because of the smell of paraffin. My favourite meal was a big pan of fried onions. When nearly ready, I would lay slices of corned beef over the top and then eat out of the frying pan, so I wouldn't have a plate to wash up.

This was the life, work if you wanted to, sleep any odd hours, fish or roam the great heath, beachcomb when the winds favoured. I was much in demand. Residents could get no one to do odd jobs, as chaps would not travel the five miles from Poole, so I could pick and choose whatever job I wanted to do. This way, I got to know who was a good employer or otherwise. But I also met some very funny ones; including the old Scottish couple – mind, they paid me very well, but did they study economy? Not half.

They would save matchsticks; when they had 400, it was enough to light one fire. And on another occasion, when I was hoeing under the gooseberry bushes, the old lady came out and counted every berry.

'Do you think I would eat any?' I hinted.

'No, but you might knock one off and bury it.'

I would be told to come to the door when I had done exactly £2 worth of work. She would then pay me £1 19s 11d and say, 'You won't have to put a tuppenny stamp on the receipt now, so we've both saved a penny.'

Time and again she would say, 'When Mrs C goes out, stick the fencing posts about three feet on to her land.' When I went to Mrs C's garden, I would be told to put the fence back three feet. This happened a score of times, but it was easy work re-fixing the posts, as the sandy soil was soft.

One day, a three-day sand storm from the north-east completely buried the old Scots' bungalow up to the eaves, the sand coming from a high dune at the rear. It took me four days to dig 'em out, and I was bad with sand in my ears and throat for a week.

A Miss W asked me to call in one evening and carry a case to another house, so I knocked at her door at about 6.30 p.m., waited while she packed the case until 7.40 p.m. and then took the case. On my return at about 8 p.m., she said, 'Now, let me see, you've been gone twenty minutes, so I have to pay you fourpence as I normally pay at the rate of one shilling an hour.' Yes, I've met 'em all. Missed my tide home, too, that night.

I suppose I could have been called a "sandscape" gardener. Isn't it wonderful how people can grow things in pure sand and fair rainfall.

With there being no school on the Sandbanks peninsula, the children had to be rowed across to the school on Brownsea Island. There were only a few of them and these belonged to the coastguard. This twice-daily row was an arduous one when the tide ran strong and gale-force winds raged.

The lure of fishing and the great heath began to attract me again and I slept more often at the hamlet.

As I was starting off to Swanage one morning, a native came up and said, 'One of us be pinchin' my fowls, missed two yesterday; tell a copper to come over.'

That evening, two officers came on their bikes; one was the fat sergeant who had stopped me with my lump of oak. He was soaked, having fallen into the stream when he had tried to ride over a narrow wooden bridge. The natives turned out to gaze upon the strangers. Then, to avoid being charged, they offered home-made wine to both men, who, getting somewhat fuddled by the drink, could not make head nor tail of what was amiss. They then mounted their bikes and wobbled away. But the fat sergeant, now soaked both inside and out, went head over heels once more into the stream.

Going to Swanage a week later, I saw the sergeant at the same road junction. He beckoned me to come over.

He said just this, 'Look here, young man, don't you ever come here again and make a complaint about that lot o' lowlanders out there, they can dang well murder themselves for all I care.'

Discreetly, I did not pass on this information.

At one point I was away at sea for four months. On my return, I found that someone had broken into my cottage and a watch and some books had been taken. There was little else of value that appealed to the intruder; I said nothing to my naughty neighbours.

9

Tam is Launched

For some time now I had been using one of Stephen's boats, so I was very pleased when my own boat was ready to go afloat.

I had enough money saved to pay the full amount of £17 in cash, with a further £12 for extras, such as oars, anchors, mast and two sails, etc. My large sail was tanned and waterproofed; the smaller sail was a storm one for heavy weather.

Tam proved to be everything I desired. She was easy to row, would not capsize and could be hauled clear of the breakers by using rollers on 6-foot slats of wood. I was now to begin a long period in my life that was to prove most pleasant, excitable and rewarding. Thousands of miles were to be covered in sailing her out to Swanage Bay (nine miles) or to Studland Bay (seven miles). In these bays, I began beachcombing, often finding a great variety of most useful things. These consisted of money, jewellery, timber such as fifteen-foot deals, mahogany hatch covers, blocks of pitch pine and crates that had fallen off the decks of ships. Within three years, I had picked up about £280 in coins and rings, pearls, bracelets, earrings and oddments to the value of £250. Now I had no use whatsoever for the money I picked up, nor for the cash I received for gold or silver articles, I just had the urge, the satisfaction, the thrill of 'combing the long, lonely shores when trippers had long-since vanished as each October came round once more.

The Shell Bay and Studland shores are composed of very fine particles of sand. When a strong wind blows from one quarter for two or three days, the sand is blown before it. This lowers the shore level by many inches, so that any coins, shells, bits of coke, etc., remain poised upon a conical cone of sand – like a golf tee. But even then, the discoloured coins are not easy to see as so much other litter is revealed at the same time, so one has to become really expert at one's job. It is the glorious uncertainty as to what you may discover next that keeps you with eyes downcast on a windswept shore when all the other folk have left the scene. I've wasted two hours searching and only found tuppence before now. Another time, I picked up over £4 in under an hour.

One November saw a terrible south-easterly gale, which widened the mouth of the harbour entrance by forty feet, and part of the shore was lowered by four feet. Revealed beneath was a bed of black peat and on this surface were a number of old coins; they were pure, untarnished silver and dated back to the sixteenth century.

Sometimes, I would go over to the Bournemouth seafront. Here, it is only worth beachcombing during the autumn and winter, or when a gale was sending huge waves up the sloping shore. As each wave runs back, coins are revealed for a split second, before a watery sand hides them again. You have to be quick – follow the receding wave, grab your coin and dash back as the next big wave comes surging in. I know longshoremen there who have found rings varying in value between £100 and £850. Visitors to the shores in the summer lose an enormous amount of money, children especially. These coins easily slip into the dry sand and it is not until the autumn gales come that the treasure would be uncovered again. Rarely did I see anyone on the shores of Shell Bay in winter, but one such day a gent approached me, curious to find out if I had lost something. I explained what I was doing and as I did so, I noticed the milled edge of a shilling. I asked him if he could see it; 'No, nothing like a coin, but there's a lot of shells, corks and bits of dead seaweed.' I bent down, removed the shilling, raked the immediate area with my fingers and found three florins and a second shilling. Where one coin is lost, one can often find others. Fellows who lie on the sand in the summer do not realise that money trickles out of their grey flannels and vanishes under the sand.

My boat Tam became most useful for going ashore where timber had been washed up. My voyages to the tow bays and other sections of coast were not only for beachcombing. Curlew, otherwise known as the haunted house, had been a keeper's cottage many years ago, but it had now become encircled with brambles and was surrounded by tall firs, the branches of which brushed the windows in rough, windy weather.

There was no path leading to the place, it had long-since been lost in the heather, and the nearest road or habitation was three miles away. If you struggled through the brambles you could walk right in, as the door had also long-since vanished.

On turning left to enter what was once a sitting room, you would receive a severe shock – there, in front of you, would appear to be a real, live Indian. It was actually a life-size drawing done in coloured chalks upon the north wall. The fellow was dressed as a chief and was seated before a fire; in the background stood a wigwam and dark green fir trees. Strange writings were on other walls in the Cree language. Proceeding up the stairs, you would come to a notice which read: "He whoever entereth here will have his head choppeth off".

In a small room was a mass of dry heather. This had at one time been a tramp's bed, but he had disappeared a few years ago. I had known him when I had first visited the great heath; seems he had been in Canada for many years before coming home to England and he, like me, had roamed the heath. It was he who had done the drawings of Indians, hoping it would scare any intruders from the place, as he lived in Curlew. The old fellow was known as the "Wild Man" back in those days. Funny thing was though, I became known as the "Second Wild Man" as time went on – perhaps I deserved this title.

I had first met my counterpart back in about 1914, when I first began to dig bait at Shell Bay. He would approach me and ask for about a dozen worms, which puzzled me, as I'd never seen him with a line before. So, one evening, I watched as he went round Bramblebush Bay. He went over to a large gorse bush and pulled out the framework of an umbrella from a clump of heather. On the ends of the ribs were hung some fishing hooks, which he baited up. He then walked out to the low-water mark with the contraption and stuck the handle into the mud, leaving the circle of hooks just clear of the ground. He told me later that he would go out at the next low water to retrieve any fish that had been hooked. His average was two flatfish, but one day, a big bass nearly carried the umbrella away, only it became stranded as the tide dropped.

I never knew this fellow's name, nor I suppose did he know mine; perhaps it was because I had so many names both good and bad. My normal signature was B. B. Pond; the initials stood for two long

Christian names – Benjamin Baverstock. But I've also been known as Jim, James, Ben and the Wild Man, amongst others. Names in the press have been B. Pond, Estuarian, X.Y.Z., Bernard Pond; later, I was most surprised to be addressed as "The Duke of Goathorn". The word "Goathorn" was related to a mile-long peninsula, which jutted out into the harbour and was covered by dense woods. I was given the name "Jim" from Stephens, when nine of us were doing a rush job on a large vessel. In fact, anyone who worked for him was called by that name. On that particular day, Stephens was in the chart room when he had called out, 'Jim, bring me a hammer.' As we had all been addressed as "Jim", all ten of us proceeded to the chart room, each with a hammer. We never heard the word "Jim" again.

10

Meeting Marconi

The Haven Inn at Sandbanks was but a small place back in those days. Its only customers were the local pilots, the ferryman, a few coastguards and, believe it or not, smugglers. I would pop in for a drop no more than once a week; the beer is so watery, give me real rum or brandy any day.

The host was a Monsieur Poulain from across the channel. A most excellent fellow, who was keen on catching mullet, so he sometimes came fishing with me. Mind, he could tell some tall yarns; one morning I was in the bar when he was describing a big fish he'd caught near Le Havre. I can see him now as he said, 'De moullet was as long as this, look.' Then, with arms fully extended, he turned towards the door. A very stout woman was about to enter, but, not expecting such an affectionate welcome, she retreated and thirstily went on her way.

Signor G. Marconi was often seen at the inn. His steam yacht Electra of 900 tons would be anchored to the south of Brownsea Island castle. Many of Marconi's experiments in wireless transmission were carried out in this area.

I remember one particularly glorious summer evening when I pulled Tam ashore, as I would be sleeping in my hut that night. A short little fellow, not too well dressed, approached and asked, 'Could you put me aboard?'

I knew him to be Marconi, so I hesitated, then remarked, 'But my boat is all muddy, been out bait-digging.'

'I do not mind,' he answered, so I pushed Tam back into the water.

As I rowed him the 200 yards out to this magnificent floating palace, I was much puzzled. Why did he ask me to do this when there were four boats on the davits and two more alongside the companion ladder, with a crew of fifty-eight aboard?

As we reached the yacht, in a low tone, he said, 'I shall have to stop my men buying your bait.' And, winking an eye, he gave me two five-shilling coins – a huge sum in those days.

You see, I had earlier sold the crew some worms, and they were all so busy fishing off the stern that they clean forgot about the boss. Did he stop me selling his men bait? No.

I continued to beachcomb and long-line in the two bays, when a funny thing happened near the old wreck in Studland Bay. Noticing a large crate that had been washed ashore, I waded in to collect it, when a fellow in only a bathing dress came running up. He was in a panic and blurted out, 'What am I to do? My clothes is all burned and I got to get back to Parkstone. Must of dropped 'em on me fag-end. I can't get on a charabanc like this.'

He was nearly demented. Now I always carried a reserve of togs in the forward locker, so I fished them out, giving him a torn jacket and a pair of very shrunken trousers. He put these on and started off for the ferry. He must have had quite a job getting those tight trousers on; in fact, he must have been the very first beatnik ever seen on the Dorset coast.

Later in the winter, when 'combing amid the sand dunes, I came across the ashes of his clothing and a few buttons. Raking the sand beneath the ashes, I found sixteen shillings and fourpence, so I was amply repaid for my old garments; he must have forgotten his money in his fright. I believe I got eight bob for the crate as well. In fact, it was quite a profitable day, with 28 lb of fish too.

Gradually, more and more trippers started coming over on the ferry. Picnic bottles began to accumulate, some of which would be broken, and so I collected the pieces as they are a danger to bathers, children and dogs. But by dusk, the trippers would have left on the ferry and I would be the only living thing that might cross the great heath at night; the old tramp had long since gone.

I had been to Bournemouth one day and had arrived back at Sandbanks late. The tide being adverse, I decided to leave my boat at Shell Bay and walk the four miles over the heath to get home. It was very dark that night as I trod the narrow black peat path, bordered on either side by tall bush heather. I had gone almost a mile and was nearing Bramblebush Corner, when I saw something white in my path, about seventy yards ahead. I stopped, and then moved slowly on – must be a large sheet of newspaper, I imagined. But the paper, or whatever it was, moved slightly, yet there was no wind. I stopped dead in my tracks. I was now really scared, alone on the great heath, where not a living thing should be. I was unable to continue on my way. It moved again, so at last, I decided to move out into the heather and make a wide half-circle. When I got level with the object, I saw that it was only a white donkey; but worse was to come. I began to laugh at my earlier fears and regained the path farther on, then stopped and looked back at the donkey. As I gazed back, the animal was no more – seemed to disappear into thin air. Surely it could not have gone behind the bramble bush, which was forty yards from the track. Again, I became scared. I shivered and hurried on my way. Reaching my cottage, I turned in but slept little.

Morning came and I had to return that same way. Surely I would not fear anything in the daylight. Reaching the bush, I searched all around it for hoof marks; they would be clearly evident on the soft peat and the sandy patches. But there were none, not a trace of a donkey's hoof-prints. Never in the darkness did I pass that way again; instead, I always kept along the shore. I even made enquiries for miles around – quite a lot of crofters had donkeys, but none owned a white one.

Some time after this I was in the Bankes Arms at Studland and in chatting to an old fisherman, I told him of my scare upon the heath. For a minute or more, he said nothing, and then he looked at me and said, 'So you've seen it, too?'

Apparently, he said, 'Must be fouwer on us as seen the donkey. Same place, too. Same time o' night, nigh midnight, I saw it back along as I comes round that way. I wus thic afraid I never came this way agin. Old Bosanquet saw it, so did Fryer – you can 'member he, a winkle man. See, 'bout 1780 or so, a feller was ridin' a white donkey on his way to Wareham wiv a cash o' rum an' a bag o' silver. 'E gets to wer the brambles be now wen 'e was set on an' killed by a smuggler, round 'bout midnight. The donkey ran away, so 'tis said, but 'e come back. I can tell you the very day an' month as you did see it, 'twer twenty-third o' December. And nigh midnight fer shuwer,' he added.

I was amazed, the fellow was dead right; it was 23 December and around midnight, too. Until I heard this story, I had never given much thought to ghosts, spooks or apparitions. For further proof, I went and found the winkle picker. He, too, confirmed having seen something, but said it looked like a human being. This may have been because the donkey was "end on", just as I had first seen it, but he did not get a broadside view like I did, as he was so terrified that he had returned to his boat and awaited daylight.

Beachcombing was still adding many things to my store. I had been going to Peveril Point once, when a wooden bedstead of all things came floating by, and I thankfully hauled it aboard. Until then, I had been sleeping on the floor. In my living room was stacked one and a half tons of clean-washed coal that groundswell had heaved ashore.

Odd hikers and the natives used to stare, open-mouthed, amazed at the variety of strange objects within (including me), as they pressed their faces against my windows. The BBC tried to reach me with a recording van once, but got stuck in a bog and thought better of it. Had I succeeded in finding a set of three brass balls, I could have opened the finest pawnshop in the south of England.

I kept my wooden bed in the back room, along with stacks of oddities, including one under the said bed.

11

Haul of Ten-shilling Notes

One afternoon, a gale with driving rain sprang up, so I made for the Haven Inn. I lingered there for a while with two pilots – you could have a drink any hour of the day back then. My appearance was not very presentable: my coat was of the Egyptian fashion – all rubber, no buttons, only flick-over metal fasteners, and the collar was velvet; my hat was a lifeboatman's type, in black and red.

After a while, the door opened suddenly and in came a tall and most handsome fellow. Then, looking at me, he exclaimed, 'Good heavens! The Duke. Yes, the Duke of Goathorn.'

The title was to stick to me for a long time, even on letters addressed to me that came through the post. I had not seen him since pre-war days.

'Where you been hiding all this time?' I asked.

'Been over the States, rum-running. Prohibition has ended, so decided to come home.'

Yes, this was Captain Collins, ex-navy. We had been fishing together before the war and now he boasted a magnificent black beard, which tapered to a point ten inches below his chin. We talked for some time about the past few years and then I got up to leave, but he pushed me back in my seat and called out to Poulain for more drinks.

'Look here,' he began, 'I want your help, partly as a witness, but also in the future. You see, you know these local tides and coast, and what's more important, who's who. Will you meet me at the gates of my father's house at Salterns at three o'clock on Tuesday? Now here's a fiver. You will?'

I took it and held it up to the light, and then he glared at me and said in a loud voice, 'I made over £10,000 in less than two years over there, you'll see just what I shall do with it.'

I was at Salterns as arranged on the Tuesday, when he turned up in a wreck of an old Ford, minus one mudguard. Inside the car were four sandbags, all apparently full, of what I had no idea. Taking two bags each, we marched straight into his father's study. Not a word was said as the captain untied each sandbag. Then he proceeded to empty the bags, littering the room with thousands of ten-shilling notes. At first, the old gent was dumbfounded; as was I.

It was the captain who began to talk first by saying, 'Now look what your son has earned. You know all about stocks and shares, I want you to invest all this, 19,800 ten-bob notes. I've got enough to go on with and to form a towage and salvage company.'

Now his father was quick to realise that his son had not earned all this money by the sweat of his own brow, so the money was put into an investment that only produced one-and-a-half per cent per year, for a fixed period of five years.

Two weeks later, when Captain Collins found out that he could not get back the capital for at least five years, not to mention the low interest rate, he came to me saying, 'You recall what I said to you in the inn, that I might want your help about tides and some other things? Well, at that time it had already occurred to me to form a towing and salvage company and by heaven we will do it in a big way now.'

He did just that. He got fifteen fellows to join and invest about £300 each, put in £1,600 himself – I, too, paid in my fair share – and we bought a 400-ton trawler, complete with various small craft and gear. We were all surprised though, when our captain also bought a large speedboat costing about £2,000. She was mahogany, with diagonal planking and double skinned, twin engined and weather screened; at that time, she was the largest and most powerful craft of her kind to come into service so far.

Soon, we began towing with the trawler – the *Shifter* as we named her – but jobs were few and far between. Sometimes, we took yachts from one harbour to another and at other times, we steamed up and down sections of the English Channel, where we might find a brig or schooner in need of a tow on a windless day. But our *Shifter* was very, very slow. In fact, on one or two occasions, the trader asked us if we wanted a tow; seems we could not raise enough steam on the kind of coal we had.

If the captain was absent – as he so often was – I took command, and I soon began to feel very unhappy. My crew began to grumble, because wages were not paid promptly. Also, the cooking arrangements were anything but ideal. At last, I tackled our captain about this problem, and what a surprise, he handed me nearly £800 in fivers and pound notes (no, he had not been to a bank for ten-shilling notes this time). So I was able to satisfy the crew by paying back money and also two months' wages in advance. Later, at Falmouth, we had improvements made to the galley and a raised tow bar was fitted.

We returned to Poole two months later and were laid up for five weeks. The hull was given a coat of paint, as were all the other craft. On most nights during this period I was able to sleep at my cottage on the heath. I even thought about going back to my simple way of living, and the life I loved so much. One night, I had gone to bed when someone knocked on my door. Who could it be? I wondered. Getting up to see who it was, I discovered that it was none other than the captain himself. He was in a most distressed condition and he spoke frantically.

'I've been searching this vast heath and woods ever since two o'clock to find the Duke's Palace. Now weary and footsore, at last I stand before His Grace.'

He was deadbeat and must have walked many miles, so I got the fire going with fir sticks and boiled a kettle on it for some tea.

'What have you come for? Is there a mutiny aboard?' I asked.

'No, nothing like that. I really must have your help tomorrow night. You must be west of Martello Tower from six till eight. When you see two flashes in succession from a green light, you must reply with two flashes of blue light, also in succession, with this torch.'

My two blue flashes would mean it was safe to enter the harbour. If unsafe, I was to signal at least a dozen flashes.

'But whatever is the reason for me doing this?' I demanded.

I listened intently to all he had to say. He talked for a long time, explaining why I was to be at the tower. He also revealed that he had already made two such trips across the Channel with the speedboat, loaded up with rum and brandy, landing one lot at Warsash and another on Lepe Beach on the Solent. If the coast was clear, he intended to land a third load at Redcliffe in the Wareham Channel.

Local officials and some of the Harbour Board would already have left for Weymouth to bring back a tug, and they should be out of the way for at least forty-eight hours.

The captain went on, 'But there is a risk that fellow Riggs may not go to Weymouth and if the customs launch is back in the water after its overhaul, he may well be pottering around in it. I believe he has some notion or other as to why I got this speedboat. Anyhow, if you can find Riggs' whereabouts as I near the shore and you think he might be afloat, I need you to give me a dozen blue flicks with your torch.'

'You must know more about local doings than I do,' I broke in.

'Well, I've been nosing around just in case. Another thing, I did not want to get you involved, but now and again I may well be glad of your help. If it's at all unsafe, I will go on to Warsash.'

I then told him that rumours were going about and that the fellow Riggs had actually asked me why we had bought such a costly boat for our fleet. At the time, I had explained that I did not know, and that it was for passenger use if a BOT licence was eventually granted, perhaps.

Sleep seemed out of the question, so we talked until dawn, at which point we walked to the shore and crossed the harbour in Tam. I was unsure what to make of the whole affair, so I spent the day fishing; no other pastime is so pleasant.

12

The Captain is Caught Red-handed

I took 40 lb of bass that day, but there was no time left to go round selling the catch, so I sold it on to two fish hawkers.

Just before 6.00 p.m. I reached the Old Martello Tower, which was on the top of Canford Cliffs. Visibility was not too good, darkness was setting in and a fresh wind had started to blow from the south-west. Making myself snug in the bushes, I began my vigil. Torch in hand, I gazed seawards into the increasing darkness. Seven o'clock came round and no green flashes. Then eight o'clock, and still no signals. The sea was getting increasingly rough, with big waves crashing against the foot of the cliffs. By the time nine o'clock came, I decided that surely the captain's boat could not be out on a sea like this; he must have stayed on the French coast, or perhaps made for Warsash in Southampton Water. With these thoughts in my mind, I went back to Tam, sailed home to my cottage and turned in.

Now, before I relate what happened in the next forty-eight hours, I must describe the coastal border of this south-west side of the harbour. Earlier, I referred to Goathorn Peninsula, which extends a mile out into the harbour. This long neck of land is mostly covered in trees, but a light railway runs through them from Corfe Castle, terminating at the end of the peninsula where there is a wharf, from which clay is loaded into sailing ships. An ancient little L & S W Railway engine would pull about a dozen trucks, each containing three tons of clay, on this lonely journey of nearly ten miles.

The next day I set off to the wharf, near to which Tam was moored with two of my other boats. Emerging from the trees, I was surprised to see a barge at anchor; there was also a tug across the narrow channel, which was hard aground on the mud. It was all a mystery, with no sign of life aboard, as I sailed past on my way to Sandbanks.

As I neared South Haven Point, I had another surprise; there was the speedboat at her moorings, with its forward windscreen smashed. Where was the captain, what had happened?

I could find no news of him, so I set sail from home early in the afternoon. Reaching the tug, I went alongside and climbed aboard, just out of plain curiosity, or perhaps some strange urge or other. Bottles were scattered about the deck and two half-filled crates were in one corner. Peering into the cabin, I saw a number of prostrate forms, but there was also a young fellow seated and dozing. I attracted his attention and called to him to come up on deck.

'Tell me, is this a booze-up, am I seeing things?'

'We caught your boss last night, he's for it. We had been to Weymouth to fetch this tug back. We was supposed to have brought her back today, but as a gale was likely we decided to return early yesterday. We was passing Kimmeridge 'bout five o'clock, when we received a Morse message to tow off a barge, which had been moored in under the cliffs to load stone. She was pounding pretty bad. We had to bring her on to the Goathorn Channel, using two ropes parted, due to the swell. Then we got a heavier warp aboard and had just reached Handfast Point, when your boss comes alongside. He was in a terrible state, soaked, windscreen busted, and his boat was very low in the water, because he was loaded with casks and crates of spirits. Had to hail us to save his blessed life.

'We humped up nearly 200 lots of the stuff to lighten the boat to save her from sinking. Then we towed him to harbour and cast him off, as we had enough evidence on board. Also, we had to leave the barge up Sou' Deep, near the wharf, before we could go on up to Poole Quay. We moors the barge, takes too big a circle in this narrow neck and goes aground. They be all drunk as they could be, down below.'

Then an idea came into my muddled brain.

'You carry cameras, being sometimes on survey work, would you have any now, this being a new vessel?'

The fellow looked hard at me, then said, 'There they be on that locker seat, but what's it matter to you anyway?'

'It do matter to me. You won't be mixed up in this. Here's three quid, more if my plan succeeds. All you have to do is take a few snaps of this lot sprawled on the mate; I'm no good with a camera.'

The bribe worked. Taking several pictures at different angles, he then took out the film and handed it to me in a canister, just as some of the fellows were starting to stir. There was no time to waste. Hopping back into my boat, I hoisted sail and with a fresh wind, made for Poole.

Here, I found a chemist that I knew and asked him to develop the film as soon as he could – sixteen from each negative – telling him to come to the quay when they were ready, as I would be waiting at the steps all night. No wonder he looked a very puzzled man.

If the tug got off on the evening tide, my plan was ruined anyhow. By being at the quayside, I would know if they came ashore. The long, dark hours hung terribly slowly. By 2.00 a.m. I felt sure that the tug had failed to get afloat.

Was I glad to see that chemist? He came along at about seven o'clock and gave me the package. All the photos were good, five different, sixteen of each kind.

Another long wait ensued and it was nearly noon by the time the tug tied up and the gangway was lowered. As each man came slowly down on to the quay, I handed each one five different pictures.

'Less said the better,' I remarked.

You should have seen their faces and heard their mutterings. Not a bottle was to be seen on the deck, but plenty of empty ones drifted in and out of the harbour with the tides for weeks. When I did run into my captain, he told me how he had given up hope that night.

Then, seeing the tug with the barge astern, he'd had no option but to seek their aid.

Then I told him my story. He was amazed, but it wasn't until I produced five of the photos that he believed me. After that, we celebrated; good job nobody took any photos of us.

Having sobered up a bit, we went to the top of Brand's Creek. We landed and then walked over to where four cottages had stood once a long time ago.

The captain began, 'Do you recall telling me of this place, that there were two wells by an old orchard? You said that smugglers used to hide their spirits in these wells. Well, that's exactly what I've done now with the cases I still had left on the speedboat. As soon as they cast me off that night I came on up here. Thought to meself, you won't have

47

everything I had aboard. Thanks to you, I wasn't charged. Let's sample a brandy and make a resolve – no more smuggling in Poole Harbour, we go east and get tobacco off a Dutchman instead.'

He offered no further explanation, but a week later, they took our Brixham fishing boat and a flat-bottomed punt to Southampton. I did not go with them, but the captain and three others went for four days. It wasn't long before I discovered just why they were in that region and what had happened.

The Brixham trawler had to be eight miles south of Niton on the Isle of Wight at eight o'clock one morning, in order to contact a Dutch trader and receive two tubs of tobacco of 90 lb each in weight. Due to some error, no contact was made and the Dutch ship came up Southampton Water at about 10.00 a.m. with the tobacco still on board. The skipper sealed the two tubs, dumped them overboard and took cross-bearings.

Later, our captain went to the ship and saw the chart, on which were marked the spot where the tubs had been sunk with weights. So the Brixham boat began to trawl the area; it so happened that the local fishing fleet was just setting off on the tide. Seeing our boat going round in circles, the fleet thought we had found the fish, so soon there were seventeen boats also going round in circles. It wasn't long before one of the boats fished up a tub, and then another got the other one. But our boat had no more legal right to the tobacco than they did – just another case of "less said the better".

13

Midnight in Curlew Cottage

I spent an hour in the haunted house now, as it was known then. Yes, Curlew Cottage, where no one had lived for a great many years, except for the old tramp, and that was some years ago, too.

It so happened that I had been to Bournemouth one evening to visit my sister, having sent her a postcard earlier asking her to do some shopping for me. Leaving her house at about 9.15 p.m., I walked to Sandbanks some five miles away and rowed over to Shell Bay. As the tide would be against me if I went home by water, I moored up Tam and began the four-mile walk over the heath, taking care to avoid the place where I had seen the white donkey. A storm seemed to be not far away and dark clouds had spread in over the harbour sky and darker still lay the lonely heath.

Nearing Curlew Cottage, heavy rain began to fall. Here, surely, was shelter. I did not want my food and papers to be spoiled, so I crawled through the tangle of bushes and entered the cottage, going into the first room on the left of the passage. Sitting in a corner, I flashed my torch on the inner wall, lighting up the perfect life-sized drawing of an Indian chief. I shivered; it was as if his eyes were fixed upon me. Hastily, I put the torch back in one of my bags.

The rain was falling in torrents and a terrific wind was blowing, causing the branches of the tall firs to sweep against the outer walls. Flash after flash of lightning came continuously and as each brilliant flash came through the window, it lit up the Indian. His eyes were staring straight at me. I was sure that his lips spoke; maybe the thunder and noise of the gale drowned his words. Somehow, I moved about two yards from my corner, but still those eyes were fixed upon me as each flash lit up the scene. I was afraid. No, more than afraid,

49

I was terrified. As I sat shivering – and not from the cold – my thoughts drifted back to the night when I saw the white donkey, but a mile away from this awful place; thinking of this made me even worse.

Perhaps I ought to have been thankful for this shelter from the raging storm outside. Why did I not go to my hut in the dunes at Sandbanks instead? I looked at my watch as the next flash came, it was just past midnight. Surely those two eyes were fixed upon me, yet I dared not look directly at this Chief of the Crees; only from the corner of my right eye did I keep a wary guard.

The next moment, there was a loud thud from the room directly above my head. I half rose, and then fell back in panic. Vivid lightning lit up the whole room – the Indian seemed to be enjoying the storm, despite the fierce look on his thin face, enhanced by high cheekbones. Then came another thud in the room above. It was too much, I could stand no more. So, struggling to my feet, I grabbed my things and dashed out into the raging storm. In my mad rush, I dropped much of my shopping, as it got caught up in the brambles, but I dashed madly on all the way back to my cottage and arrived soaked to the skin. Changing into some dry clothes, I slept "all standing" – if you could call it sleep. Those eyes, those two thuds, were so deeply impressed upon my mind.

Two days later, one of the natives of the hamlet came to my door with some butter and eggs. We talked for a while and then he suddenly remarked, 'The old tramp's back up Curley. Come back 'bout twelve day ago.' The chap looked at my startled face, 'What's matter?' he asked.

'Oh, nothing, I just dodged into Curley to get out the storm the other night. The old fellow could have been upstairs same night, heard two thuds, might have been when he took his boots off.'

A day or two later, I met the old tramp near the ferry. We chatted for a while, and then he suddenly exclaimed: 'Had a terrible fright night o' the storm. Somebody stumped out o' room below. I'd bin in some time, never thought anyone was down in Cree's room.'

Then I told him my story and you can be sure that we both had a good long laugh; after all, it all seemed so funny.

'And what's think you, ther' wus parcels o' grub outside, what you must 'ave left. It wus proper beachcombin' on my doorstep.'

That same day, I went to Wareham and bought the lightest pair of boots I could find, depositing them at Curley on the way home.

Some months later, I ran into old Peter Cafe. He was nearly eighty and had sailed all around the world in windjammers. We called him "Kaffey". I told him about the white donkey, also my night in the so-called haunted house.

Then I asked, 'Do you believe in spooks, ghosts?'

He was silent for a minute, and then began, 'Course I do. See, every Christmas, I 'ave a drink at every pub on the quay. Then, feelin' sort o' 'appy like, I turns up high street to go 'ome. Wen I gets to marine stores I do see two figureheads up over, instead o' one. She must 'ave a twin sister as on'y comes to see 'er wen it be Christmas. Funny fing, ain't it?'

I entirely agreed.

The "training bank" was a bank of rocks that took about a year to construct and it extended one and a half miles seawards from the north end of Studland Bay. Most of the rocks at its base weighed about ten tons each and were brought round from the Dorset cliffs by barges when sea conditions permitted. The upper layer of rocks graduated from three tons to three hundredweight, and was brought to Goathorn Wharf by the light railway, which also loaded clay on to the sailing ships.

The reason for erecting this rock barrier was to prevent the ebb tide from the harbour turning into Studland Bay. Thus, the whole force of the tide was confined to the fairway by this long training bank, and it was so directed to wash away the outer sandbar. Ships drawing 18 feet can now come into the port of Poole two hours either side of high water.

Away from all the formalities and worries, the noise of traffic and the crowded streets, these past few years I've lived a free life. No politics, no bills to pay, no clock, no hawkers at my door. Perhaps I really was becoming the Second Wild Man of this great Studland Heath.

What a wonderful panorama lay before me. Miles to the south, the range of Purbeck Hills rose to 700 feet. To the west was five miles of undulating heath, then, by turning towards the east, a long fringe of sand dunes topped by waving marram grass could be seen. Beyond, lay the open sea, where, on a clear day at some fifteen-miles distant, the western end of the Isle of Wight was visible. To the north lay Poole Harbour with its five islands, three of which were densely wooded.

I now realised what a carefree and healthy life I had; the few natives supplying me with the best of food, and any money I earned at Sandbanks or found on the shore, I began to save.

Always keen on wildlife, I enjoyed watching the many kinds of birds. One day, I found the nest of a black grouse with six eggs – how odd, they are only said to nest in Scotland. I also found a quail's nest complete with eggs. Redstarts, stonechats and wheatears all build their nests in gorse bushes to avoid the snakes, as adders and grass snakes won't go after the eggs, because of the sharp prickles. Most of the smaller birds feast on sandhoppers, of which there are million on the sandy shores. Curlews, oystercatchers and sandpipers feed on the mudbanks in the harbour at low tide. Over the years, I recorded 240 kinds of birds around the harbour, the woods, the heathland and Littlesea Lake; some of these I could not identify, I am no bookworm.

With the exception of certain occasions, I had not worn boots or socks for several years and my feet had become hardened to walking barefoot on pebble beaches and through the heather. It was a marvel that I escaped being bitten by an adder – though I was twice stung by a grass snake, but hardly felt it. Many snakes lived on the great heath, the adders being mostly around the fringes of Littlesea Lake.

A green mossy bank comes to mind, where, on a sunny day, there would be at least a dozen adders and grass snakes, even a smooth snake. I had got so used to seeing natural life that I was content to live with it and never so much as destroyed even the adder, which eats thousands of mosquitoes.

14

Learning the Hard Way

There are many books written on angling. These may be of some use to the fellow that only has infrequent opportunities to fish, but if time is not a handicap, then it is far better to learn by trial and error. Luckily for me, I had the time. And in doing so much intensive fishing in so many places and at all months of the year, I came to find just when and where the best of my sport would be. Yes, I learned the hard way.

I can recall going off in Tam for a long day at sea, 14 miles from the shore. Dropping anchor, I filled my pipe after lowering a line. As I was about to light up, I dropped my matches into the bilge water; no smoking for the whole day. Had the *Olympic*, the largest ship at that time, come along, I would have stopped her and begged for a box of matches. Since then, I've always carried two boxes. In some 38,000 miles of sailing alone, I have learned to take many things with me: compass, Morse lamp, riding light, spare anchors, ropes, sails, rowlocks, change of clothes, chocolate and rum; yes, rum. And it was thus that I was prepared for trouble or to go to the assistance of others, to tow home craft with broken-down engines or to pull people out of the water, never coming to grief myself – mind, I had some near squeaks, but don't we all during our lives?

The most delightful angling I ever had was on the Whiteground.

This was a long spit of sand situated between many mudbanks, in the south-western part of the harbour. I would anchor off the end of the spit just after low water during summer evenings. Here, one had the music of the small waves breaking over the sand ridge when the prevailing westerly wind blew. Away to the south lay the vast purple heath with a dense copse or group of firs here and there at the foot of the Purbeck Hills. What a vast expanse of wild and unspoilt harbour-side lay before me. With not a human being in sight, it all seemed to belong to me.

Dropping two lines over the stern, I would get fish after fish: bass, plaice and flounders. Within two hours, I would have a bag of sixty or more pounds in weight of choice fish. But I had no market in which to sell my catch at that time, so all the fish were given to the natives farther round the shores or to those nearer to my abode. In return, I received vegetables, fruit, butter, milk and other things. On rare occasions, I took the fish across to Poole, getting two or three pence a pound. This money, along with some of my beachcombing coins, went on tobacco, bus fares and picture papers, which I took back for those on the heathland.

I had now drifted farther away from Collins and his crew. Seldom did I go to sea with them any more, although I heard that there was still much discontent among the men, with wages always owing. But I was to have two more spells afloat with him and his men.

A lovely day in April found me once more aboard the *Shifter* for a six-week spell of towing jobs. With the exception of towing a brig, which had lost both masts, we did not get another job, although we cruised (or drifted to save steam) for many a day. Payment for this solitary tow would be made in July. We were all a bit browned off, the food was all gone, we had not washed for weeks and the water allowance was just one pint a day.

By mid-June, we were just off Durleston Head and on our way back to Poole, with our fuel almost exhausted. Missing the harbour tide, we hove to in Swanage Bay, our total cash assets being just two shillings. For this sum, we could at least get tea, sugar and fresh milk; all the tinned milk had been used up a week ago.

One of our hack boats (a ship's lifeboat) was tied astern, so we all climbed into her and rowed to the pier, where we landed and went off into the town. After purchasing the said groceries, we marched back on to the pier. We must have looked like a wild, motley lot. We put the fourpence left out of the two shillings into the RNLI box, much to the surprise of the pier officials, who didn't have the nerve to ask for pier tolls. What wonderful cups of tea those were.

At midnight, we came into harbour with the tide and tied up on the Hamworthy side. Later that day, our captain sold a quantity of towing hawsers and other gear, paid us some of our back pay and then sent us all home on leave. Perhaps the thing I enjoyed most on that trip was being able to fish in distant waters when not under steam, mainly south of Ireland. There, we found black bream weighing up to five pounds, whiting up to four and a half pounds and many other species of fine fish. In fact, we practically lived on fish.

Having been home for about a month, I met a local fellow in Studland. He began talking about a party of shipwrecked sailors who had come ashore at Swanage. 'All darkies they wus, knees sticking through ther' trousers, tough lookin' lot.'

I had a hunch just who those chaps must have been, and asked, 'Did the leader have a pointed black beard?'

The fellow replied, 'Aye, 'e did, so they said.'

No wonder we were referred to as "darkies", none of us had washed for weeks due to a water shortage. Coal dust had done nothing to improve our appearance either.

For the next couple of years I became known as the Wild Man of the Heath, No. 2 again; the old tramp being No. 1.

Late one summer evening found me fishing beyond the bar, three miles out to sea at about sunset. I had been catching dabs when a big fish began to take my fish off my hooks. Searching in my forward locker, I found my old conger line of 60 lb breaking strain. Baiting with one of my dabs, I lowered the line to the bottom. Soon, something began to move off with my tackle.

It did not put up much of a fight, yet I struggled to bring it up from the bottom. Several times, I got it up to within a few feet of the boat and then it would bore down again. Twice, I got a glimpse of the thing – must be a skate or ray, I decided. Still the battle went on into the night, until at last, or so I thought, I could row and tow my prize ashore.

Hauling up the anchor, I tried to do just this, but, instead, the monster was towing me out to sea. There wasn't a soul in sight on this lonely sea to render a hand. Using both hands, I regained a few feet of line, and then the line broke. It had frayed on the gunwales; the strain had been too much. Sadly, I sailed for harbour and for the hut at Sandbanks for the night. I dare not tell the story, nobody would believe me. No, I had no proof; best to forget all about that lonely night on a lonely sea.

But, of course, you can't keep an event like this to yourself for long and a month or so later, I happened to be chatting to one of the local fishermen and was soon telling him of the tussle I'd had with the monster. With a queer look in his one remaining eye, he gazed hard at me. Another unbeliever, I decided.

Then he blurted out, 'Look here, if you go round to Syd's place he might have summit of yours.'

Sure enough, he had. Whilst trawling outside the bar, he had fetched up a skate of 178 lb. And that's how I recovered my trace and hook, still attached to the fish. I still have that bit of tackle. Odd things like this only happen to anglers; it's no wonder that it is the finest pastime in the world.

15

Old-time Sailors

Many brigs, schooners and three-masters came to Poole during my years on the heath. The quays would be crowded with sailing ships from foreign parts, but few of these vessels had auxiliary engines; they depended upon their sails.

Goathorn Wharf had its share of traders for clay, but the depth of the water would only permit loading of up to 400 tons. To complete the load, the ship would have to go on round our harbour to Poole in order to take on more clay. It would take about six days at the wharf to load a cargo. What, you may ask, did the crew do in the evenings? They could not be in a more isolated place, with no roads for miles and no shops or entertainment.

One day, the captain of one of these ships asked me if I would take him across the harbour to Poole, so that he could complete his papers and also do some shopping. We sailed across in Tam, taking a course between Furzey Island and Green Island, through a network of narrow channels that lay between hundreds of mudbanks. The captain was amazed that we did not go aground. I told him that I had got to know the harbour pretty well and as Tam did not draw much water, it was possible to sail over most of the banks when the tide was full.

He began to feel more at ease as we sped along, and said, 'I see that you've got a boat or two inshore of the wharf; one looks like an old ship's lifeboat, could you take my crew over to Poole for an evening ashore?'

So that same day, I went aboard and told the crew to be ready at 5.45 p.m. and that we would return from Poole Quay at 10.45 p.m. After that first trip, I made many similar ones, taking the crews inland of most of the ships that lay at the wharf. If the wind wasn't favourable, we used four cars, the journey taking between sixty and ninety minutes according to route. Should the tide be very low though, we had to follow the twisting channels. The crews were mainly those from the north continental countries, with a sprinkling of British, also a few Russians and Greeks.

The hardest part though was to collect the fellows in Poole for the return journey. There would always be one or two who would get drunk, which might mean that we were held up to search for anyone missing at return time. I found that the Russians were the best-behaved men, never had too much drink and always ready to help row the boat. The vast network of mudbanks extending over many square miles of the south-west and west parts of Poole Harbour make navigation difficult and, with a boat drawing two feet or more, one has to keep to the narrow, twisting channels. This is fairly easy in daylight, as posts mark your course, but if fog prevails or you are out on a dark, misty night, you may well run into a post before you see it, and even then you may not know on which side of the channel you are. At night, one is apt to dip the oars deeper. If the blades touch the bottom, you know that you are in shallow waters. When you know the set of the tides, with the alarm note of a startled sea bird or the rattle of a mooring buoy, in addition to lowering the oars, you can manage to avoid getting grounded on a mudbank.

The captain of a British ship paid me ten shillings for a trip, which was good money back in those days. Crews from the foreign ships would give me tobacco, bottles of beer or even fish and chips in exchange. I still had little use for money, but found myself earning more in various ways, such as pulling yachts off of mudbanks and towing broken-down motor boats inshore. This meant that I was getting less work from our Captain Collins, as I found plenty of other things to do, so I did not bother to go to sea with the *Shifter* very often.

Sandbanks was growing, more houses were being built and a regular bus service was set up from Westbourne. Also, three more roads were constructed amid the sand dunes. More trippers came over on the ferry boat, but only a few of them penetrated far over the great heath. The Haven Inn had not only been improved, but greatly enlarged. Things were changing rapidly, though not to my liking as you may well guess. The wild natural beauty of Sandbanks and the south-eastern side of the harbour would soon be no more. Though my little hut among the sand dunes was still hidden away, being on the private grounds of the Irish lady, so I still had my safe retreat.

An ever-increasing number of craft were being moored off the north shore, known as Stoke's Lake. They were all kinds of shapes and dimensions and the owners – all of one mind – had the urge to install engines. Yes, engines of a sort, which they obtained cheaply from old car breakers' yards. The age of motive power had arrived. Most of these craft had seen their better days and many leaked like a basket, as they were never intended to take the weight and vibration of engines.

How I always detested engines – the noise, the fumes – give me a sail or pair of oars anytime. They were more economical, more pleasant; I didn't even like the modern types of boat. Very few of these boat-owners ever got away from their moorings, as they were unable to get the engines to run for any length of time. Most evenings and weekends, the owners would be aboard fiddling with the levers, gaskets, flywheels and whatnot. After hours of tinkering, a voice would come from across the water, 'Jim, lends us a boat.' And so it came about that I increased my fleet of boats to six.

After many months, some of the owners of these craft actually cast them off from their moorings and proceeded out to sea. Seldom did they get far though, before the engine would conk out. I would then have to go after them and tow them home.

Come 8.00 p.m. I usually set sail for Goathorn. As I was about to set off, someone would invariably say, 'Will catch you up and give you a tow.' But as I sailed on, I would look astern, and what did I see? One of those crocks having already broken down en route, so I would have to put about and tow them back to their moorings. Most of them carried neither oars nor sails. It was possibly what I saw on that shore that caused me to hate anything mechanical; never have driven a car or been the owner of one.

I had many a laugh at the activities of these "Summer Sailors". Come October though, they would all be gone, their craft hauled up until April. But by May, they were once more afloat.

One chap, a tall, thin bank clerk, had bought a wreck and had installed a heavy, old car engine. The first summer, he never even got the thing to fire up at all and then, the following year, one Sunday morning, the engine actually began to splutter and make strange noises. The din and pungent fumes lasted for about twenty minutes. Some people close by were just about to sit down for dinner on their houseboat, when the noise and fumes drifted through their windows.

'Could you move farther away?' the lady called out.

To which the lanky bank clerk replied, 'It would be easier for you to take up your two-ton anchors and shift.'

Then the engine finally packed up.

The fellow yelled out to me, 'Jim, bring me a hammer.'

I pushed off and handed him my brand new hammer. He began bashing the machinery to pieces, bit by bit, and then, all of a sudden, my new hammer that had cost all of four shillings and sixpence sailed out of his hand and into the sea, never to be seen again. He offered to reimburse me, but I would not accept anything, having enjoyed the spectacle from the shore. Go to the pictures? Not me, there was plenty to laugh at nearby.

16

"Mine Adrift!"

Captain Collins came up to my lonely cottage one evening imploring me to come back for a while – just a simple job to be done in the Solent later in the week. Rather reluctantly, I agreed.

Then I hinted, 'Not much wages for the gang, can't go on like this, when will you pay the back money?'

'We shall pack up end of next month, sell the jolly lot and share out,' he replied. 'I may have a buyer for that little sailing dinghy of mine. Lady Paula is at Canford Cliffs and she's on the lookout for a small craft. She's coming down tomorrow.'

The next day, I happened to be near Stephen's Pier. The tide had just about gone out and moored off the end of the pier was the sailing dinghy. Two people were looking down into the boat, some twelve feet below. It was Lady Paula and the captain; he was telling her what a wonderful little boat it was.

She did not seem much impressed, so then he suggested a demonstration, which he did – not half – he jumped from the high pier down on to the bow of the slender craft. The stern shot up into the air and the boat did a complete somersault, while our demonstrator went head first into the drink. She turned, said not a word, hastened back to terra firma and we saw no more of her. But I did hear later that she had gone and bought a house at Shaftesbury – 700 feet above sea level.

I joined some of the gang three days later and we sailed to the Solent in the Brimham trawler, towing a flat-bottomed boat. We had orders to fish for flounders near the mudbanks during the night. Then, just before dawn, our captain would arrive from across the channel with a load of winkles. Now why in the world would he want to import winkles, when tons of them went from Poole to France?

None of us knew the answer; all we had to do until he arrived was to be sure to catch some fish.

This, we did, catching a fair number of fish. The captain did not arrive until about thirty minutes after dawn.

'They may have seen me come by Hurst Castle,' he remarked. 'Quick, get the trays ashore before the tide gets too low on the mud. While you're doing that, I will go well out into deep waters and drop over this here big football, which will drift westwards on the ebb. Then one of you must run along to the coastguards and tell 'em a mine is adrift, to make sure the coast is clear.'

Meanwhile, we took the thirty-five trays to the New Forest and loaded it onto the lorry – well, all except one tray; this, we kept for ourselves. Under the top layer of winkles were three rows of brandy, three bottles in each row. Sure enough, the coastguards had their telescopes trained upon the black football as we got on and finished the job of unloading. This fellow who had given them misinformation, a Londoner and a bit of a daredevil, actually went back to the coastguards' boathouse and put a full bottle of brandy inside the door at the end of the job.

Later, I heard what became of this load: it went to certain inns in South Wiltshire and North Hampshire, the winkles being sold over the counter well salted. This created a great thirst, which, of course, meant that the customers called for more drinks. The reason why we had caught the fish was so that any earlier suspicions were not aroused.

Some weeks later, all our craft and gear were duly sold as the captain had said. There were still fourteen in the party and we shared about £120 each, so in the end we never recovered our full investment, which just goes to show that smuggling does not pay. Maybe watches and pearls pay better.

I returned to my normal fishing, looking after boats, with a bit of beachcombing and a weekly cycle ride to Parkstone to visit my sister, who was glad to have a bit of fresh fish, in-between. Rarely did I don boots or socks, never collar and tie, and I still remained free from the petty frivolities of town life. I also still had no clock or watch, as I had no need of either of them.

It was now 1925, which saw the coming of a new road that was built across the heath from South Haven Point to Studland. Luckily, it only infringed but slightly inland and was about three miles long. But this road crossed the old track by which local natives could get to Studland, so I protested and we were given a free right of way; other users had to pay a small toll. To connect this new road with Sandbanks, a steam floating bridge was instituted. This could carry both cars and their pedestrians wishing to get from the Sandbanks side to Studland or on to Swanage, or vice versa.

More and more people came over to South Haven on both the steam ferry and motor-boat ferries, but most of them stayed on the sands at Shell Bay and did not venture far inland. In some places, the bush was dense and interspersed with bogs, meaning that hundreds of thousands of tons of stone were needed to go into making a foundation for this road, owing to the boggy nature of the subsoil. Part of this road passed near to the north end of Littlesea Lake and the noise of passing cars caused the gulls to desert the area.

Until then, 2,500 pairs of black-headed gulls had nested there, the nests being so close together that a small triangular depression existed between every three nests; each nest contained three eggs, or at least it should do. But the birds squabbled among themselves so much that odd eggs rolled out of some of the nests into one of the triangular depressions. I never had to rob a nest, as I could always fill a basket of eggs by collecting those which had rolled out of the nests instead.

One day, I was asked to go in a cabin cruiser for a long day's fishing trip to the west of Lulworth. It was a twenty-eight-foot craft, which I had assisted in building. But never mind about that, we very nearly put the "finishing touches" to it off St Alban's Head. For the maiden trip, I took charge for the owner and with six jolly pals we set off on the seventeen-mile trip. Also on board were cases of beer and several bottles of whisky and gin. I could see trouble ahead, I'd had similar sorts of days before.

Reaching our destination, we caught some fish in the first few hours and then the bites became less and less frequent. The party got very merry; bottle after bottle was consumed. I was handed glass after glass, but chucked the contents overboard – I had to keep my senses about me. By about 4 p.m., I decided to get going, as a nasty sea was getting up and wind forces were increasing from the south-west. It took nearly an hour to get the engine to respond, but at last we moved off. When about a mile offshore from the rocky coast, we broke down. Heavy seas caused the boat to wallow as we lay broadside on, drifting towards the rocks.

Soon, we were within eighty yards of the shore, when the owner of the boat stood up, waving the starting handle around his head and singing *Britannia Rules the Waves*. He was too drunk to realise our peril, as a breaking sea caused him to lose his balance and the starting handle went flying into the sea. Masses of black rocks momentarily appeared amid the boiling white foam. Then I remembered putting a box of odd tools aboard (half expecting trouble) and in it I found a thing like a bed key. With this, and another chap swinging the flywheel, we actually got under way and steered out to sea for at least two miles in order to get clear of the dangerous coastline, eventually arriving back at Sandbanks. I had to carry one gent back to his house and the others were so badly affected that they forgot their fish, which I had divided up into equal numbers, so I had the lot, plus the deposits on the empty bottles.

It was the only time I ever sailed under the New Zealand flag, the boat owner having some interest in that country, so we carried four stars on the blue "duster".

17

A Fishing Competition

I did not bother much about time, so I did not carry a watch. The one I did have, some time back, had disappeared from my cottage when away at sea. It had been admired by a nearby neighbour and I had a strong suspicion that he was the fellow who had taken it; however, to remain friendly, I did not accuse him.

Occasionally, the captain lent me a watch when there was a specific need, but the last time I was with him he presented me with a brand new wristwatch, saying, 'Thanks again for those snaps you got, also the two wells in the old orchard.'

There were occasions though, when knowing the time was useful, such as when a Mr Hobday suggested that we joined the Parkstone Angling Club, so that we could go in for a competition. Being a professional, I was only admitted to the club on the condition that I did not sell any fish I might catch. On one particular day we all met at the club hut to go fishing in our boats from 10.00 a.m. til 4.00 p.m.

'You, come with me. We are not going to the usual marks such as the Rock or the Wreck, we are going alongside Middle Sands, buoy twenty-nine, opposite Evening Hill, got your watch?' I asked Mr Hobday.

'No, don't take it fishing. What you got those three boxes of sand for?' he asked.

Proudly showing him my watch, I said, 'We shall need to know the time, so that we pack up in good time to weigh in – oh, the boxes of sand, you'll see later.'

'To weigh in, you seem pretty confident,' he remarked.

Reaching our mark, down went the anchor and a handful of sand. Every now and again, over would go some more sand, and, now and again, one of us would land a nice flatfish. And so it went on, until about 3.15 p.m., when it was time to go back to the club hut. Instead of three boxes of sand, we now had nearly three boxes of fish.

This was not too good a catch to my way of thinking, but Mr Hobday seemed delighted, saying, 'I see now how a cloud of sand will bring fish to our lines.'

We were the first to get back, but waited for all the others and let them weigh their catches first, us being new members. Catch after catch went on the scales, but nobody had more than about 2 lb 6 oz. Finally, we put our catches on; we both had similar weights, nine and a half pounds of flounders and eight and a half pounds of plaice each. Combined, our totals exceeded the catches of all the other twenty-nine anglers. We not only took first and second prizes, but we shared the sweepstake too, and I gave all my catch to the coastguards nearby. Some of the members appeared quite annoyed at the results, so this was the last time we competed.

I am not against competitions in general, but I dislike tiddler snatching, which is done to add weight to the bag. Many of these young fish are weak and are not yet fully developed, so they are bound to suffer injury when hastily unhooked and thrown in a keepnet and jammed in with scores of other fish. It's about time that a minimum size limit was brought into general use. Any fish, no matter what its size, should be killed if too badly hooked; such fish, if put back in the water, become diseased or eventually die.

I suppose I was like the Lone Ranger, glad to get away from things – give me the undulating heath and the rolling sea any day.

I now began to spend much more of my time in Swanage and Studland Bays, trotlining, digging razorfish and beachcombing. Tam proved the ideal boat for every purpose: rowing, sailing, heavy seas or beaching when huge groundswells rolled shorewards. Never would I have survived with any other kind of craft, but, having pointed ends fore and aft with crown decking, I could run through the big shore rollers and any waves at sea.

The training bank had now been finished and stretched one and a half miles out to sea from the north end of Studland Bay. This proved a nuisance to me, as I had to go at least one and a half miles extra when entering or leaving the bay. I decided this was not good enough, so I borrowed a crowbar from Stephen's boathouse, then, choosing a day when the tide was low and the sea fairly smooth, I prised off much of the upper layer of rocks, until I reduced the bank level by some three feet in depth, and to a width of fifteen feet. I had to make it as wide as this for a safety margin when heavy seas were breaking on the rocks. This shortened journey was to save much time; also, on dark, stormy nights, it was difficult to locate the far end of the bank.

The southern end of Studland Bay is terminated by Old Harry Rocks. Inland is Ballard Down, 700 feet in altitude, and the extremely pretty village of Studland lays at the foot of the hill. Most of the bay has a wide shore of excellent sand, inland of which are sand dunes covered in marram grass. After the dunes lies the great heath and dense copse. A mile to the west on a forty-foot high hillock is the Agglestone, a huge rock of over 400 tons. No one knows just how it came to be on this kind of pinnacle, but local legend has it that Satan picked it up from near Tilly Whim Caves, intending to drop it on Stonehenge when a religious service was to take place. Finding the Agglestone too heavy, Satan had to let it fall. Wiltshire natives say that the big slab of stone, lying at an angle near the circle, was also dropped short of its target by the Devil. Another huge white stone lying in the Hampshire Avon is credited to the Devil, who failed to reach Salisbury Plain with it.

Sandbanks was now becoming a popular resort for outings and Sunday-school treats. Children would not leave the boats alone; sometimes, they untied anchors and away went a boat on a rising tide. It got so bad that I bought an old wreck of a large yawl and made this available to all the youngsters; at least it saved damage to other craft.

One morning, some school children on an outing crossed over to Shell Bay on the ferry as I was bait digging. I happened to look towards the point, when I saw my big boat drifting away out of harbour on the fast ebb tide, full of children. They had pulled up the anchor. Soon, they would be on Hook Sands, where huge seas were breaking.

I ran to the point, jumped into Tam and went after them, reaching the big boat just as she neared the breakers. Making fast, it was useless to attempt to row and tow against the ebb. I had to row across the tide, eventually being carried a mile down the coast. Here, I left both boats and walked back with the fourteen youngsters, who had lost three good oars. When I found the schoolmaster, I was rewarded with half a crown for saving these young lives and losing three oars.

In my time, I've rescued and pulled "out of the drink" nearly fifty persons for an average reward of one or two shillings and threepence. Makes one think, doesn't it. I rescued a girl swimmer once, exhausted and clinging to a barrel buoy that had just been painted with black and white stripes. She had "stolen" most of the wet paint and looked like a zebra. Needless to say there was no reward, her purse was elsewhere – not that I expected one. Out of the many craft that I've towed home or assisted in some way, seldom do they offer a tip.

The only time I reap the benefit is during the winter, when drying winds blow the surface sand on to the dunes after loose coins have fallen from the fellows' grey-flannelled pockets.

One summer, a party of girls rowed down from Poole to bathe in the nude at Pilot's Point when evening tides were favourable. News of these visiting mermaids reached Bournemouth and from this pier, the paddle steamer would make its daily, single trip back to Poole, its passengers returning to Bournemouth by tram or train. The steamer soon became crammed with young fellows with field glasses and cameras. One trip had such a crowd on board on the port side as the ship approached the scene that it listed, causing the rudder to come clear of the water, and the ship veered straight for the shore. The girls fled for the sand dunes and somehow, the captain managed to go full speed astern and the fun was over.

The police were informed and the excitement came to an end. But since that time, a nudist colony has been opened near Studland and strange things have been seen in the air. They call 'em helicopters.

18

Ashore and Afloat

Another night, I had to walk back over the heath to my cottage. The hour was late, but I was determined to avoid Curlew Cottage, the haunted home of the old tramp. He would not be at home anyway; he had gone away to Cornwall some months back. Apparently, he intended on staying down west for a whole year, right over the winter, which was going to be a severe one.

Drawing level with the lonely house, but still some distance from it, I glanced sideways towards it. A light shone through the thick undergrowth, which was in front of the very room in which I had been on that stormy night. I stopped abruptly. Who else but me could be upon this deserted heath at this hour? Sheer curiosity drove me to investigate. Crawling through a mass of foliage, I got to within three yards of the room. In it, I could see at least seven men, all seated round an oil lamp. I recognised two of the fellows: one, a crofter from the Corfe Castle area; another, a winkle picker from Poole.

Moving into position, I eavesdropped on their conversation.

'Then this is the last lot.'

'Aye, I don't want to get copped, things be too hot.'

'We can't hide casks in Littlesea now; that keeper gets around there more since shootin' bin let.' There was a pause as drinks were passed round from a small barrel, then the crofter said, 'I can't spare the time to drive to Blandford again, I got me cattle to feed. Somebody else must clear this load.'

'Look, this load that's coming in on Saturday night, what say we stow it for a while, could do wiv a cask meself if nothing else.'

'If we don't put it into Littlesea come Saturday night, why not get it round to Redhorn Quay or Brand's Ford, could hide the stuff down the old wells there?'

Then the winkle picker joined in, and what he had to say gave me quite a shock.

'We've already decided to use Jim Pond's big boat. I knows the way 'tween the mud up to Brand's Ford; we can use his boat to get there. At least we can depend on his boat, as it's always moored at South Haven weekends, in case he gets a Sunday party for fishing. We've used 'er afore, twice, and he never knew.'

'And lets leave him a drink in the stern locker, we owes it to him,' someone added.

'Well, that's it, midnight then.'

A couple of the fellows got up off the floor, so I cleared out as fast as I could go. Reaching home, I decided to leave my own boat for their use, if only to get the promised drink, brandy, whisky, which?

Hastening to South Haven on the Sunday, I went to the boat and peered into the locker. Sure enough, I found several bottles of beer, how I detest the watery stuff. Then I had a brainwave. Later that day, I took the beer with me and went to the old wells (where Captain Collins had hidden some of his load some time back). Putting the bottles of beer into the well, I took, in return, a cask of tip-top brandy.

They must have been mightily astonished as to how I knew what they had been up to, also to know where they had hidden the load.

Sailing ships were now definitely becoming fewer in number and more and more steamships were coming into the harbour. During the month of August, however, three sailing ships came to the wharf for clay. During that particular month, I made about eleven trips out to Poole with the crews.

Being on the quay for long hours, I noticed a lad of about nine or ten years of age, who wasn't playing with the other boys. Each time I saw him he would be seated on the Custom House steps all on his own, whilst all the other boys were on the quayside, fishing. It seemed odd that this boy did not join the other lads, so I asked "Jo Jo" Brown, a pilot, the reason why.

'Oh, he's afraid of the water, can't bear to look down at it far below, funny kid,' was his answer.

Taking another party over again the next evening, I noticed that the boys at the quay were catching flatfish as usual, when one of them trod on a slippery fish and went fourteen feet down into the water below. Everyone was horrified, no one moved, except, yes, except for the lonely boy.

He dashed across the road, dived in and reached the boy, but it was futile, both lads were drifting away on the ebb. Mr Stokes, a seaman, and I rushed into the water and reached the lads, bringing them to the steps fifty yards down tide. Never again was the lonely boy taunted about being afraid of the sea. We are an odd lot; we've just got to change our way of thinking sometimes.

Some time back I had got to know certain fishing areas through going out with Mitchell-Hedges, the explorer and big game and fish hunter. These grounds were situated in the western end of Poole Bay and we caught some really big tope, conger and dogfish.

According to my diary: "The bearings for the Middle Poole Patch of rocks, keep Swanage Pier open Boscombe Pier were NE 16 degrees E and the Chalk Cliffs W 29 degrees S. There should be three fathoms HWOST, and I supply this information for the benefit of visitors who are going after big fish. To find the Yards, keep the Agglestone over the coastguard's old cottages, bearing 76 degrees W, in line just clear of Redcliff, drop anchor due north of The Yards, depths varying between 3–4 fathoms H.W.O.S.T." But I got tired of catching these big, ugly fish – and nobody wanted to buy them – so I went back to catching choicer species.

One moonlit night when sailing back to the wharf, I was tempted to lay a trotline at the end of the Whiteground spit. Keeping the mooring cork in alignment with the moon's beam on the surface so that I knew where to recover the line, I did just that. After about forty-five minutes, the cork buoy began to bob about in a most curious way and then began to move off, so I quickly went after it. Hauling it aboard, a fish on almost every hook, I noticed that a conger eel had been hooked, too, and it had twisted the tackle up into a ball. The heads of all the fish tied together resembled a stem of bananas, which was impossible to unravel, so I took the lot back to my boathouse, where I cut up the line and counted my catch. There were seventeen whiting at a pound apiece, three flounders and a 15 lb eel. Only four hooks failed to take a fish. It was a most unusual catch, as whiting rarely come into such shallow water in that part of the harbour.

Here's a tip about trots: never lay them across a strong tide, because if there is a lot of drifting weed about, it will carry your corks under. Also, never set a baited line at the low-water mark, as seabirds might become hooked.

About a week after this, I happened to get a heavy bag of fish, mostly flounders, so I loaded about 60 lb onto the carrier of my bike and cycled to Wareham to find some buyers. It would perhaps be wrong to say that I cycled the eight miles, as for five of these miles I just had to push the machine, as the going on the heath was so bumpy. I soon sold the fish and I retired to the inn by the river bridge. It wasn't long before I was in deep conversation with an old native; he seemed to know everybody's business for miles around. I pushed a couple of pints in front of his mouth and this started him off talking again.

'You don't know George, I suppose? Well, one night he went home and said to his wife, "Can't make it out, there bin a bike up at the fishing hut all the week, donno who it can belong to?" His wife at once suggested that he should go and find out if anything was amiss. Perhaps the owner had drowned?

"Good lor' yes, he could be, best go and search down banks," says the worried man. Anyway, he goes to the shed to get his bike – no bike, it was his own bike that was up at the hut. You do meet 'em, you know,' my storyteller added.

For a while, he stopped talking, but somehow I had an idea that he had not finished his story.

Continuing with our conversation, the old native said, 'See that out there? Well, that there be George's bike.'

'Where is he then?' I asked.

'Oh, he went home on Saturday, must have forgotten it.'

'When will he come back for it?' I enquired.

'When he goes out to his shed to look for it, I suppose.'

Moral: When going to the waterside, don't forget anything. When returning, don't leave anything behind.

19

Harbour Freezes

While we are alongside this Dorset Frome, it is worth recording the weights of some of the fish that have been landed.

A lady, fishing alone, caught three salmon in one morning – all over twenty-nine pounds each. Major Radcliffe had one, a forty-nine-pounder. Also taken here were two of the record sea trout, both weighing exactly twenty-one and a half pounds each. The river also holds specimen dace and roach.

In November, a really cold spell set in. It was the worst I had known on the south coast and it made me think back to what the old tramp had predicted just before setting off for Cornwall; he was right. The month began fairly cold, but by about 10 November there was a heavy fall of snow with three frosts. By 15 November, most of the snow had begun to disappear; however, by about 19 November, we had continuing frosts night and day. On the third Monday at 4 p.m., I recorded that it was only three degrees above zero. Never before had such a low temperature been known to occur during the daytime; even the harbour began to freeze. As the cold spell continued, so the ice became thicker; only the three main channels remained free of ice, and this was only due to the movement of shipping.

Every morning, I had to cut a channel through ice to reach open water, a laborious job taking an hour or more. Not only did I have to keep my own boats from being crushed, but there were several others at Sandbanks which I looked after for their owners. With the exception of when breaking the ice, I was still going about my business minus boots and socks. Each day, when first going out, my feet would tingle, but after about ten minutes I was all right.

I had bought several strings of onions from the French boys, without bothering to beat them down on the price – they had jolly well earned it. Filling a large pan with chopped onions, I fried them until three-parts ready, and then added slices of corned beef and completed the frying. I ate it straight out of the pan, tasted better that way and there was also no plate to wash up afterwards.

Many square miles of the backwaters of the harbour were now frozen to a depth of four feet. Trouble was in store. One particular day saw a very high tide, lifting vast areas of ice. Some of it broke into small portions that began to drift with the ebb tide in other areas, flowing as much as a mile wide and in length, weighing a thousand tons or more. Yes, this spelt trouble. Hundreds of posts which marked the secondary channels were knocked over and craft were set adrift, as the floes cut through the iron mooring chains like a knife; this sounds incredible, but it's true, nothing will hold against a thousand tons of ice, which bears down on a fast tide. A pilot's cutter was moored north of Stoney Island; on board were many books of mine. The ice not only cut the chain, but it also cut right through all the bow planks and the boat went down, taking all my books with it.

Before the break-up, I had managed to haul ashore about thirty craft and five of my own. Only three of the owners put their hands in their pockets, and not very deep at that. Back in those days, looking after and baling out boats was a very poorly paid occupation. During heavy weather, I've been known to be out all night rounding up craft which have broken adrift; the owners, snug in their beds, never realised what the work entailed. I always had to have spare anchors and ropes in readiness for all sorts of incidents. Some of these "summer sailors" fail to realise the fury of the late-autumn storms.

Less than eighty years ago and situated almost in the centre of the large harbour, Brownsea Island had a population of 250, but since the pottery industry dwindled and the farm ceased to exist, many natives went over to the mainland. Famous families have been owners of the island, living in the castle. Today, it is controlled by the National Trust, but permits can be obtained to go ashore.

Until 1925, the Van Raalte family owned the island. They had a big staff; even had their own band, a nine-hole golf course and school for the workers' children. Services were held in the church, the parson walking the four miles from Studland to South Haven. Here, the ferry boat picked him up and took him to the little pier. I knew the gardeners, the carpenter, the butler, the boatman and others, as I often sold fish to them or took some of them over to Poole. The horses and carriages were kept over at Sandbanks. Twice, I slept in the heather on the south-western side of the island, being unable to reach the wharf in exceptionally bad weather. Large areas of the island are covered by trees and dense undergrowth.

You may wonder who owns the vast Studland Heath. Well, it was given to the Bankes family in recognition of Lady Bankes' defence of Corfe Castle. The Bankes still own all the heath and much more land around. But it comes under Settled Estate Law, which commands that a certain acreage must be maintained, for instance, they can sell a portion only if they buy five-sixths elsewhere. The inn at Studland is named after the family – The Bankes Arms.

Sandbanks, for many hundreds of years, remained a desert of sand dunes with no human habitation. The first family to settle there was a branch of the Stoke family, who came from Lilliput, three miles away, nearly 400 years ago – the last of the descendants left Sandbanks in 1924. Incidentally, this was no relation of the Mr Stokes who aided us in getting the two boys out of the water at Poole Quay.

Funny how places get named after people; a bay just inside the harbour is known as Stokes Bay. Some years back, I began calling a point near South Haven "Gravel Point" and it is still known by that name to this day. With the help of the carpenter on Furzey Island, we cleared the silt from the two small channels. One of these is today called Carpenter's Inlet – the other one Pond's Creek. Then there is Court's Folly in Studland Bay, which got this odd name in rather an odd way. I went with Mr Court to the bay for a day's fishing. When it was time to partake of the midday meal, we moved over to the sand dunes, where the said gent accidentally sat down on his lunch bag. Two of the supposedly hard-boiled eggs made quite a mess. Ah, where are you now, my old friend?

Of two chalk pinnacles, which once stood in the sea near to Handfast Point, one has almost disappeared; they were known over the ages as "Old Harry and his Wife". The name "Old Harry" still denotes the tall sentinel which now stands alone. There is a small cave in the

Ballard chalk cliffs, and it is only approachable by water. The temperature inside it is often as much as ninety degrees, even in winter. No one, so far, has found a solution to this mystery.

20

Go-to-bed Cottages

Before the coming of the steam ferry and new road, what do we know of the past history of South Haven and Studland Heath?

If you stood on the Sandbanks side of the harbour mouth and gazed across the water towards the south-west, the west and the north-west, there wouldn't be a house in sight, only miles of heathland, copses and forests. Even today, the scene remains unchanged, except for two huts and a small tea cabin. With the Settled Estate Laws in existence, it will never become strewn with houses and nor does this area lend itself to development, owing to bogs and large sheets of water.

Beneath the road to Studland are the foundations of an inn and some cottages. Parts of the inn were still standing when I first visited this side of the harbour. Although the outer walls were three feet thick, they collapsed bit by bit, due to rabbits beneath them. The four cottages nearby were called "Gotch a bade", which later became known as "Go-to-bed Cottages".

A century or more ago there was no regular ferry, which might mean that a traveller had to wait until the next day to get across, so he would go to these cottages and ask for a bed, hence the name – "Gotch a bade". Smuggling was rife at that time and the heath provided a good hiding place for deserters from the navy. The inn was a receiving place for butter, eggs and pork, which was shipped on board naval vessels at South Haven and taken to the officers' mess at Portsmouth. These supplies came from the crofters at the foot of the Purbeck Hills, between eight and ten miles inland. What a terrible journey those poor crofters had to make over the heath, which consisted of humps, hollows and boggy peat. Wheelbarrows were used to take the loads all the way to the inn. Usually, it was a woman that had to push the heavy load, as their husbands would be fully occupied on the holdings. These poor people could not afford to eat the pork and butter they produced, they lived on humbler fare.

These days, great fires sometimes sweep across parts of the heath, due to careless trippers lighting fires. If you walk across a burnt area, you may see the blackened remains of a wheelbarrow wheel, two feet in diameter. You may also come across the bleached bones of an animal that wandered from a faraway farm and ultimately died on the heath.

If you should find yourself at South Haven one day and want to cross on the ferry to get to Poole, it is only four and a half miles, but if you had to walk round the harbour to get there you would have to walk eighteen miles. Just inside the harbour at South Haven was once a stone jetty, as smooth as a billiard table, which served boats coming to the inn. It is now a mass of upturned stones, due to trippers shifting them to find crabs and shrimps.

Seldom did a stranger knock at my cottage door. Now and then, a hiker might call and ask for a drink of water. He would swallow a couple of pints and then want his flask filled, too; I would politely say, 'I have to fetch every drop from over a mile away.' On hearing this, he would look badly in need of another drink, so I would add, 'The Bankes Arms is only three and a half miles away.'

A yachtsman came one day with two great cans, saying: 'I've walked about two miles for water, could you possibly fill these cans for me please?'

I said, 'Not a drop until I walk a good mile to get some more; you passed by a spring containing excellent water on your way here.' He was beginning to look faint, so I said, 'Perhaps a couple of bottles of brandy might bridge the gap, quite cheap in this part of the world, quid a bottle.'

He gave me three and was gone. He must have passed within seventy yards of the well that held the brandy. Brandy to his left and Brand's Spring to his right.

If it had not been for the mudbanks which lay off our nearer shores, we lonely residents would have almost had an invasion from yachting people and it was down to this barrier of soft mud, that we were left in peace. Even at the wharf, a landing was difficult as no ladder led up to the high deck, and the twisting gulley where I kept my boats was tricky for a stranger to navigate.

But the softest of mud was no worry to me; in fact, I devised a method of overcoming this handicap. I obtained a wooden box with a floor base of sixteen inches by twelve inches and the four sides were about fourteen inches high. By placing the box on the mud and leaning most of my weight on the sides, I could push it in front of me and slide in whatever direction I wished, tilting the box slightly towards me to prevent it from pushing loose mud in front of me. Anything that needed to be taken with me went in the box.

Let's think about waves that sweep into Poole bay for a moment; as each great wall of water surges shorewards, it lifts a great variety of things up off the seabed, loose shells, weed, bits of coke; even fish of anything from four to twelve inches are lifted up. Many forms of fish food are also disturbed and exposed to fish on the feed. This process goes on, wave after wave, it all goes up and it all goes down, any slight implement towards the shore is counteracted by the sea levelling off. You may see the effect of this when stood in shallow water, for example, in bits of weed and debris; even a tiny wave lifts objects an inch or two. Waves – how they fascinate me.

Yes, cross-waves, steep waves, waves in a tidal race, green ones, any kind, unkind ones, too, that try to devour me and, of course, there are those that wash our shores clean. Waves only travel when they rush up the sloping shores. It is the force, the impulse created maybe a thousand miles away, that travels through the surface of the sea. If you watch a gull resting on the water, it is lifted high as a wave passes, and then bobs back down again, but it has not moved in a lateral direction, it remains exactly above the same area of seabed as it did before.

A barrow boy, mistaking me for a wealthy, ignorant, city gent, held out a six-ounce flounder. 'Nice plaice, sir, only one shilling and still alive.'

I almost told him what I received for my landings, and that his mingy little smelly fish was worth a mere penny stamp and that flounders only fetched half the price of plaice (this is a fact). Instead, I told him that I got four shillings a score in the fish market. Reaching the quay, I got clear of the smell of that long-since dead little fish, tore off my collar and bow and inhaled the ozone to my heart's content.

I also sniffed the brandy when I got home, as I'd had some trouble with some of them which had developed a queer taste, after having been put in casks and kegs that had been constructed from green wood. If the wood is not seasoned, it will affect any liquor, so I would transfer it into bottles to avoid this happening. It was easy to find these, as down on a nearby shore lay about forty empties, which had been washed ashore when I had taken those snaps of the intoxicated fellows in the ship's saloon.

One of my Fishing Parties at Sandbanks, Poole Harbour, Dorset.

Tam Poole:

Self-righting boat. Ben Pond could sit in either direction. A very clever idea. My 38,000 mile companion, about 1946 on Stour near Parley Green.

Ben Pond – Middle, back row.

Taken by Mr Hardie after paper chase.

A salmon caught at
Avon Castle, river Avon by
river baliffe Ben Pond.

Avon Castle near
Ringwood Hants.

Mr Ben Pond and
Mrs Margaret Pond,
maiden name Dore,
with Nephew and Son.

21

Thalassa and the Sea

I experienced a great change in my life – I no longer had the shack at Goathorn, and nor did I have the hut at Sandbanks – I had got married to a local Poole girl, a Miss Marjorie Dore. Yes, a real girl, who was keen on fishing, sailing, wild heaths and nature. What a wonderful partnership we had, with a ship as our home.

I had bought *Thalassa* (Greek name for sea) for £250. The saloon was twenty-two feet by fourteen feet and had three cabins with two bunks in each, a storeroom and a good galley. We lay on fixed moorings with a three-ton anchor westwards (this was the most exposed quarter), and a two-ton anchor to the east, with huge chains connecting the two. Our floating home was moored in a lovely part of Poole Harbour, from where we could see all the shipping entering and leaving. All around were many species of seabirds.

I still had Tam, but I had also obtained seven more boats to let out to fishing parties. Gradually, I got more custom and also built up a big bait trade, even sending supplies to the Channel Islands and Cornwall. By the end of the second year, I was employing nine bait diggers for lugworm and ragworm, while I carried on sailing out to Studland and Swanage Bays, fishing with rod and longlines, also collecting razorfish and doing some beachcombing.

My wife proved to be a good "first mate". While I was away at sea all day, she would be checking the worms brought in by the diggers, packing quantities for sale and attending to the anglers who hired our boats. Not far away was a newly built sea wall. Here, any boats which broke adrift in rough weather would get pounded to pieces, unless I could reach them in time and tow them clear; this was a tricky job, as I had to row after a drifting craft, get a line on it and tow it against the wind and the sea.

Most of the "summer sailors" had no idea what a half-gale can do. One Sunday morning, I had six of my fleet anchored out at the low-tide mark, all booked for fishing parties. During the night, someone took all the oars, rowlocks and other gear; no, it's not all profit. Good rope is costly – coils of sixty fathoms go nowhere and quality paint is expensive, too.

A young fellow of about sixteen bought a large sailing boat. For the first twelve months, he never left his moorings, and then one day, he hoisted sails and actually went for a short trip, with my wife and me watching from our deck. We saw him return under full sail before the wind, but instead of approaching his moored dinghy by coming round up to the wind, he bore down on it, reached to grab it and was pulled into it. Meanwhile, his precious boat went sailing on, only to run aground; it was all so comical that we could not stop laughing. Finally, I had to go and lower the sails and get the boat afloat again and back to its moorings.

We had been on-board *Thalassa* for about a year when I landed myself another job. A lady came and asked if I would give some navigational lessons, unpaid, to the local Sea Rangers. These were girls of fourteen to eighteen years of age and they had been provided with several craft, including a longboat. Some of them were very keen to learn, but my main problem was in getting them all present for each lesson. One evening, I put ten of the girls in the longboat, giving them written instructions to cover a defined course, to avoid the mudbanks. By ten o'clock that night, they had still not returned. By eleven o'clock, most of their parents were on the shore gazing into the night. By midnight, I started off to search the wide waters of Poole Harbour, ninety-six miles of coastline, at half tide. At 1 a.m., I found the longboat high and dry on top of a mudbank, with no sign of the crew. Soon, I heard voices. It was the girls; they had walked through soft mud to get on to Brownsea Island.

Now if you think there is anything funny, heroic or dramatic in carrying ten mud-plastered maidens, one at a time, out to a boat at that unearthly hour, well, you should think again. Perhaps you already have.

At 1.45 a.m., I placed my ten niggers upon our shore. Even their mothers didn't know who belonged to whom, and nor did I; I was past caring by that time. On top of all that, I had to go and fetch the longboat at high water later in the day. All gratis and for nothing.

Girls are funny things in boats; two of 'em hired a boat once and had rowed out about twenty yards, when they both jumped overboard. Seems a poor, lonely, innocent ragworm had crawled out from under the floorboards; more flotsam to salvage.

D'you know, as I sit here writing, I am constantly reminded how fortunate I've been throughout my life: no collar or tie, no creased or turned-up trousers, no clock-watching and no routine habits. Not wishing to be rude, I will say that some of you've 'ad it, p'raps better to say "you ain't 'ad it". 'Tis too late now, there be too much oil on troubled waters.

Often I get letters or callers, besides seeing things in the press, all wanting to know how I've got away with it all: my time with the Goathorn natives, living without money, the secret of Tam – my Norge double-ender.

I've lived and existed, some of you have existed and lived. I wouldn't be a millionaire for a million reasons – all good ones. Smuggling was but a pastime, 'combing another. Mind, I've been diddled over the years. I can remember the time long ago when an article in a fishing paper interested me immensely. It told me how to catch many and large bass. I copied it all out into a notebook – in fact, I learned it by heart, word for word – and I can still remember how it went: Now and again one comes upon projecting ledges of rock, around which the bass swim …

I immediately hastened, rod in hand, to such ledges on the Dorset coast. For days and weeks I continued in my pursuit of these many and large bass, going to ledges by the score and with diminishing expectations. Did I see a bass? Not one.

Sometime after I had read this article, I discovered the writer to be a lad of nearly eighteen years, a native of Birmingham (this town, eighty miles from the nearest coast, is in central England), and he had only once had a week by the sea and that was at Southend. It reminded me of an MP in the House, who was asked if he had ever been abroad.

The Right Honourable member replied, 'No, but I once spent a day at Southend.'

One of these young writers hired one of my boats for eight days. His best day's catch was under 4 lb and his best fish a dab, 9 oz. Six weeks later, I read his wonderful article, running to 1,500 words, of the huge bags of fish he'd filled, and also the immense size of some of the "specimens".

I was amused to read in the reports column of an old angling paper, (The Green 'un, twigged it), of many prime dabs of over 2 lb being landed at Southend; yes, it was Southend. Now a dab of one and a half pound is a specimen anywhere and is rarely taken. On the whole, anglers are truthful chaps, and it is only about five per cent who give us a bad name.

You may have heard of that famous bridge at Poole, which opens up to allow ships to pass through to the upper berths. Well, you can choose to believe the following poem or not:

The Bridge

As I stood on the bridge at midnight,
I thought of that good old song –
I stood on the bridge at midnight
(but I didn't stand there long).
For whilst I stood on the bridge at midnight
A steamer's whistle blew,
And the bridge where I stood at midnight
Divided and let me through.

The Great Fire

From the galley, we could see the northern end of Brownsea Island, two miles away to the west. One morning I saw a thin column of smoke rising from near Maryland, which is on the north-western corner of this island. In this region were many hundreds of acres of dense gorse, heather and fir trees; in fact, it was a vast tinder box. One day, a tremendous blaze started, its flames rising to eighty or ninety feet. That day, I saw little of the fire, having to set sail to Swanage to fulfil bait orders, but by the time I returned, several fire brigades had been landed near the castle, also hundreds of volunteers had gone over, but they were facing an impossible task. The northerly wind was taking the fire across the entire northern part of the island and along the western side.

By the second day, a column of smoke reached as far as central France, 150 miles distant, and I went over to lend a hand. Many cases of minerals had been landed for the fire fighters, but it was hopeless. By 6 p.m., I'd had enough, and my shoes were almost burned off. As I was getting into my boat, I was hailed by a motor-boat man; he had a press reporter aboard, who was anxious to catch the last train for London. I picked him up, shoved up the sail and took him to Parkstone, arriving just in time for his train.

The wind having now veered to the west, it carried the fire into the centre of the island, but it also continued to burn along the western shore. I again went over on the third day and was just in time to get the furniture on to the beach as the flames approached a cottage. Then, an hour later, we had to move everything again, because of a fast, rising tide – fire on one side, sea on the other.

The castle and surrounding buildings were saved, perhaps mainly due to the change of wind, but a huge area of land was devastated. Thousands of charred fir and silver birch stumps still stand there to this day. Many years must elapse before nature can rectify things. No one will ever know how that lonely part of the island caught alight early that morning. Opinion has it that a poacher had set it alight, because he had been warned not to land again.

Studland Heath has seen several bad fires, as so much of it consists of gorse, heather and bracken; burns for miles on occasions. I can recall fighting a fire all night once when I lived in the area.

Sometimes, my wife and I would sail across the harbour to Arne, where we would pick about 20 lb of blackberries, get mushrooms or rare orchids, perhaps a bag of cockles, followed by a spell of fishing. We never came back empty-handed. Those were wonderful days. We'd never even see a human being as we roamed through miles of dense copse and heathland. During the winter evenings, we rowed out to fishing marks and had huge catches of codling, whiting and flatfish. But, as I said before, my main job was to sail eight miles out to Studland or Swanage, getting razorfish, longlining or doing a bit of beachcombing. A trip like this averaged twelve hours or more.

No matter what the weather, Tam would face it. Some of my journeys home, often during dark nights, were difficult. With visibility almost nil, I had to judge where the rocks were by the sound of seabirds, and there was always the chance of a cross tide setting me off my course, or the real danger of running on the rocks of the training bank. One of my fastest return trips was when I had been to a spot just off St Alban's Head. By noon, a southerly gale had blown up; it was impossible to control my lines, so I made for Swanage Bay.

The weather got so bad at dusk that I pulled my boat ashore. The local fishermen were saying that Poole was impossible to reach, but at about nine o'clock, the wind force seemed to be less severe, so I ran Tam back into the water on rollers, hoisted my storm sail and set off. But had the wind lessened? No. When I'd got clear of the lee of the downs, I found a full southerly gale blowing. I continued on my way, completing the eight miles in just thirty minutes. It was a marvel, however, that I survived that wind and sea that day.

Another fast return journey that I did was also on a very rough night. A heavy gale had struck up that evening and I was late getting my lines up. There was no point in making for home too early, as the tide wouldn't be in until an hour later at the top of harbour, which meant that I could not enter Parkstone Bay until the water had covered the outer shallows. When I did at last get up the storm sail, I simply flew before the wind, travelling seven miles in twenty-five minutes.

Often, when there was no wind, or only a head wind, I would row out and back, sixteen miles in all. On two occasions, I did the journey twice in twenty-four hours; left *Thalassa* at 2.30 a.m., back at 10 a.m., left again at 3.15 p.m. and was back at 11.45 p.m.

There was no such thing as an eight-hour day for me. Time meant nothing, with having to work with the tides for my bait and fish. Sometimes, if the winds were favourable, I would go as far as the western Solent, or St Catherine's Point, about twenty miles distant. This would mean a 24-hour day, but I had good fishing, huge takes of bass and a fair number of plaice. A couple of these latter fish were over 7 lb each, but seldom was a bass over 6 lb.

My thoughts go back to one lovely day in July; I had got my normal number of razorfish, 450, taken up my three short trots, which had about 21 lb of fish on them, and with the tide still being too early, I'd sat on the crown deck of Tam as she drifted the two miles across Studland Bay, with my feet dangling in the water.

Some distance to the south, I observed some porpoises circling in large, elliptical rings, which overlapped one another. Soon, I could see that they were after a vast shoal of mullet. It looked likely that I would converge with the feeding porpoises as I continued to drift. Interested, I sat watching. Sure enough, there was soon a great commotion all around my boat, so I withdrew my feet from the water.

As I did so, a salmon of about 18 or 20 lb leapt out of the water, fell on my gunwale and slipped back into the sea, where two porpoises tore it into two pieces. I was both astounded and shocked. I looked at the bloodstained sea, but all was now still. They had got their prize, which evidently had been hiding amidst the shoal of mullet. Had I been one second quicker, I would have been able to grab that salmon – but I was too slow – always have been, as you may well have already discovered. Porpoises will swim to within two inches of a small boat without fear. Their average weight is fifteen hundredweight, but a really big one may be nearly a ton.

Such events as these linger in one's mind. There is much that the angler learns that the average man about town never even has the chance to experience; it is living, with a capital "L" – that is, if you have a boat and a fishing rod.

I used to go over to Brownsea Island sometimes to get two hundredweight of coarse, clean sand. It was the only kind in which I could keep ragworm alive for five or six days. Having to send so many worms by train or boat, I had to be particular in knowing that they would arrive in good condition. Some weekends, I had as many as 4,000 lug and ragworm aboard *Thalassa*, mostly to order, also 1,000 razorfish, which meant making up a hundred packages sometimes. Profits were small, as the diggers I employed also had to be paid. I made more on the razorfish and the fish I caught.

To end this chapter, here is a very old saying; you might even have heard it before:

Behold the Fisherman
He riseth up early in the morning and
disturbeth the whole household.
Mighty are his preparations.

Longshoreman

He goeth forth full of hope.
When the day is far spent, he returneth,
smelling of strong drink, and the truth
is not in him.

22

Day of the Storm

Early one Friday, I set sail for Studland with a fair north-easterly breeze, as I needed to obtain some razorfish for some urgent orders.

Yes, I was, of course, in Tam, which you have already heard so much about – my double-ender, decked fore and aft, equipped with mainsail, also storm sail and everything else you might need for every emergency.

I reached the banks and laid four short trots about eight miles out, and then ran Tam through the surf and beached her with my usual three rollers, and then cast out with my rod. My next job was a bit of beachcombing. I picked up fourteen shillings and tuppence, some driftwood, about a hundredweight of coal and a gold wedding ring. Nearby was a battered toupee, which I ignored, but could not help but think it might have been the last hat some chap or other had worn.

When I'd finished, I pushed off and hauled the trots. Poor results – three flatfish on one line, none on the other three, with most of the bait still intact. If you get a fish hooked early on a line it may attract more, you may even get a string of fish, but this seldom happens in this locality, as fish are too sparsely scattered. By midday, I was ashore again for my one and only meal. After this, I strolled inland to some marshland and picked a large bunch of cotton puffs – the wife wanted some to decorate a hat. By two o'clock it had become much colder and wind had backed to east-south-east. It had rained and I now had a nice plaice on my rod weighing two and a half pounds. I pushed Tam off and landed on the banks. It was time for some digging, which was nearly a three-hour job, as I wanted 440 razorfish.

With the tide turning, I took in the trots, revealing twenty-seven fish at this final hour; the best plaice was over four pounds, five others over one and a half pounds. These fish would be in excellent condition, due to the clean seabed and the quality of natural food, but here I must point out that anyone would be very lucky to land as many as twenty-seven these days, and they would be only half the size, due to inshore trawling.

With the wind now fresh to gale force and heavy rain now falling, the sea was not too bad under lee of the banks. To get round the far end of the training bank would mean rowing over two miles into the teeth of the gale, but by making for the northern corner of Studland bay, from which the long bank commenced, I could save this extra two miles. Here, 150 yards from the shore, we fishermen had made a cut, so that our boats could pass through at half-tide level, having prised off the top rocks with crowbars. But the tide was still too low to be able to get through this cut; besides, it would be another hour before it would reach the top of the harbour, so there would not be enough water to get over the shallows at the entrance to the bay where *Thalassa* was moored. With every minute, the gale and the sea were becoming worse. Slowly, I proceeded towards the cut, rowing with the wind over my left shoulder. It was a slow job, but I had time to waste, as the tide would still be too low to take the cut. Despite rowing, I was bitterly cold and soaked through from the rain.

I went ashore and looked round the point, from where I could see that the floating bridge had broken down midway across the harbour mouth. I had thought about pulling up my boat and crossing by this ferry, but I was barefoot – no, I could not do this, and nor could I walk the twenty-two miles round the harbour via Wareham; besides, I had never left Tam to do such a thing before.

Looking at the cut, I saw tremendous waves breaking over it – one second the rocks were visible, the next second would come a wall of water, eight or ten feet high. With the tide on my side of the rocks being eight inches higher than that on the other side, it meant that as each wave passed over, there was a surge of water trying to go in the opposite direction over the rugged rocks. The cut was fifteen feet wide, which may seem ample width to allow plenty of clearance, but with the seas sweeping the outer side at an angle of about forty-five degrees, one is liable to be thrown on to the jagged rocks to the port side. But I knew I had to take the chance; surely I would perish with cold, stranded on this forsaken shore, if I stayed here.

I again looked towards the harbour mouth; huge, tumbling seas were racing towards the entrance. I must get through. Running Tam back, I rowed close to the cut, trying to estimate the split second when I would have to pull through. Then I put on my double row of lobster corks – I knew that if Tam capsized, I would lose all my gear, fish and bait. She would probably right herself (as she had done before), but she might be battered to pieces on those black rocks. Perhaps I should ... I don't know what I was thinking.

Several times, I lined up to take the cut, but each time I had to pull clear to avoid being swept broadside by the excess tide in the bay. I was becoming desperate. The longer I delayed, the worse the seas became, and yet the wave troughs on the cut revealed the rocks, despite some rise in tide. The driving rain meant that I could not see too well. Again, I lined up. It was this time or never. Pulling like mad at an incoming sea, I cleared both them and the next few waves to avoid being thrown back on to the rocks.

For the next 200 yards, I rowed towards the south-east to combat the breaking seas. One wave came over green. Then, seeing my chance, I swung to port and ran before the gale. Once I reached the main tidal flow, my troubles were past, no need to row, I only had to keep on course and clear the floating bridge, upon which I could see one bus, some cars and a number of marooned passengers.

Reaching Parkstone Bay, I pulled up on the gravel and walked to *Thalassa* through the rice grass, my teeth chattering as they never had before, being numb from the cold and soaked to the skin. Two hours later saw me on my bike riding the seven-mile journey to Boscombe, with 200 razorfish for Mr Mollet's customers.

I eventually made a total of over 900 trips on this job and had many a rough voyage, but none as bad or as dangerous as this one; yes, we certainly earned our money the hard way back then.

A dangerous thing I often had to contend with was the heavy groundswells that are quite frequent in Swanage and Studland Bays, especially in the latter bay. This is due to the shallow sandbanks running three miles seawards.

These huge walls of water crash with tremendous force as they pile up on any of the banks.

Due to the lateness of the tide, I would often leave on a very dark winter's night. I would have to listen intently as to where one of these waves crashed, and then perhaps alter my course. The deeper water meant that they would not pile up to crash on to the banks, but on a very dark night I might soon find myself in a shallow region again, not even knowing what course to take, and yet I never came to grief. I can only say that I've been extremely lucky, as I ought to have drowned many a time.

I can recall rowing for over a mile alongside a long, shallow bank once. With the seas breaking continuously, I was unable to find a suitable spot to cross it. At last, I got desperate, and went straight for the bank. Miraculously, three great waves crashed on either side of me and I passed over in green water.

You can only see such approaching walls of water if your horizon is at sea level. When a wave is 200 yards away, it appears like a thin black line. As it gradually nears you, the black line becomes wider and wider, and then it suddenly disappears as the wave passes under your boat. Another odd thing is that anything white on the sea's surface at night is difficult to see. Lifebuoys used to be painted white, but now they are red and white or black and white, as it is far easier to find your mooring buoy at night if it is painted black.

Those ground swells may even have travelled over 3,000 miles, majestically ever onwards, only to crash and die upon a distant shore – "Even the mighty shall fall".

23

Night of the Storm

All was as still as the grave. It was uncanny and I could not rest, so I went out on deck. There was not a sound from a seabird, nor even a note from a land bird. I went along to the sailing club pier and looked towards the south. The sky was inky black away to the English Channel. I hastened back to look at the glass. It was as low as I had ever seen it at 972 millibars.

I called my wife and we took a boat each to go out and put extra anchors on several yachts and cruisers. Most of the smaller craft we hauled ashore. By 6 p.m., we had made everything snug and then Harry Chubb arrived in his naval pinnace and dropped three anchors under the lee of a rice grass island. I went out to bring him ashore.

'Don't like the look of this,' he said. 'Sandbanks is so exposed, I thought it might be better to lay up here.'

We had a cup of tea and chatted for a while about days gone by and then we went out on deck. Already, a strong wind was blowing, but we were sheltered by the rising ground to the south; only if the wind got round to the west or west-north-west would we get a buffeting.

By about ten o'clock, the wind had increased to hurricane force and was beginning to veer towards the west. *Thalassa* was pitching so badly that we extinguished all the oil lamps. From our position, there was a long open reach to the west, some eight miles in length, and large numbers of craft of every sort were moored there. Also 600 other yachts and dinghies lay just off the sailing club.

By about midnight, we had westerly wind force of 90 mph. All kinds of boats came drifting along, only to be smashed to pieces on the sea wall, which ran round most of the bay. I managed to pick up a few and tow them to shore. In running along the little pier to fend off a dinghy, I was blown into the raging sea. How I got out I'll never know, but I had to stay in my wet clothes all night.

Things got so bad that it was impossible to attempt to save any of the scores of craft as they drifted past. Luckily for us, we were in an area with a ridge of gravel windward; only a few dinghies fouled our chains. But quite big waves were sweeping over this ridge and we were fully exposed to the wind force, so my main worry was whether *Thalassa* would hold on. Would our anchors drag, or a chain break?

My wife and I stood under the lee of the saloon, it being impossible to walk on the exposed decks. How long we remained there we don't know; we seemed spellbound as we saw the tops of the waves blown off the sea and carried away for miles inland. It was little wonder that thousands of trees and other vegetation were doomed to die from the brine deposits.

The wind force was now well over 100 mph and was coming from west-north-west, but the cloud had dispersed, so we had a much better view as the moon became unobscured. We could now see about 150 craft being pounded to pieces on the sea wall. Many spectators came and went during the night. Those on the high ground had to stay flat on the ground until about 2.45 a.m., when the rapidly decreasing wind enabled them to get back on to their feet.

Slowly, the tide level fell. It had been higher than anyone could recall. At first light of day, I walked along the shore from the sailing club to the Blue Lagoon, where I picked up more than 100 oars and placed them on a wall for owners to sort through them. Offshore, I could see many large yachts and steam vessels high and dry on the mud.

My clothes had dried on me – not for the first time – and at about 7 a.m., the lifeboatmen came aboard for a cup of tea and a cigarette. They had been soaked through since midnight when they were swept onto a shallow bank and they'd had to stay there until the tide fell low enough to leave the boat and wade ashore.

Leaving us, they caught the early bus back to Poole; they'd had just about enough of it. They had been called out at about 11.00 p.m. to go to a steam yacht that had been adrift with five people aboard, but the lifeboat had been unable combat the fury of the gale and was driven ashore.

I heard later that Weymouth came off fairly lightly, but in the Poole area, more than £40,000 was paid out to boat owners by insurance companies. What the total loss amounted to, no one will ever know, as only one craft in every six was covered by insurance.

The area of the cyclone extended from West Bay to Southsea. We, at Poole, were in its central track. The Met Station at Nelson Road a few miles away estimated the highest wind velocity to be 112 mph. At 109 mph, it put the anemometer off the recording chart and Nelson Road is a sheltered position, so I'm inclined to think that in our harbour the wind force was at least 120 mph. Inland, hundreds of trees were blown down and many roofs were damaged.

No trace was ever found of several of the larger yachts, which were carried out of the harbour at the turn of tide. It was assumed they had become waterlogged and had foundered. Much of the damage and loss incurred was due to owners who didn't have good enough moorings. Their boats broke away and were swept into other craft, which also thus suffered damage.

Past records seem to show that such a cyclone as this may happen only once in a hundred years, a lesser one in fifty years and a very heavy gale in twenty-five years. From 1921, I kept daily records of rainfall, wind, barometric pressures, temperatures and tide levels. By 1935, I worked out averages and made comparisons. I found that a very low reading on the glass added thirty inches to the tide level and that a very high reading reduced the tide level; in other words, the variation was as much as thirty inches between a very high glass and a very low one. With a high reading, the tide would get low enough for me to obtain at least 450 razorfish; just a few inches difference in tide might mean I would only get half that number.

I then began to study and compare the movements of weather systems in conjunction with the barometer and eventually, I discovered how depressions affected the sea's surface by drawing water from regions that were covered by an anticyclone. After much studying of weather maps, I confirmed my findings and was able to forecast the bad flooding in the Thames Estuary three days before it occurred. I also foresaw the Dutch floods and those on our own east coast.

Later on, I approached the Air Ministry with my facts. They wanted my whole story, but would not give a receipt or guarantee of remuneration. Having had advice not to part with my discovery, I declined to part with my records. Had my findings been put into practical use, thousands of lives would have been saved along with millions of pounds worth of war material. To explain my theory, off most shores there is an outer sandbank. When landing craft have to get the men and material ashore, they must first get over these outer banks. Now, had they first studied the movements of weather systems, they would have chosen the times when there was sufficient depth of water. Failure to do so meant that the craft grounded on the banks and they became "sitting ducks". This happened on the North African coast, Sicily, southern Italy and again at Normandy. All because of a lack of an extra twelve inches of water.

My discovery of barometric effects upon the sea began to be of real advantage in many ways. These included being able to know beforehand what the depth in shallow areas would amount to, for instance, as two or three more feet of water helped in launching or hauling up craft; also, in laying or taking up moorings, in repair work toslipways or piers, in expectation of heavy weather and in generally being prepared. Irrespective of tidal levels in shallow regions, thirty inches of extra water can make a vast difference in many ways.

24

Gypsy's Warning

About a week after this cyclone I received a letter from Muggy, begging me to come to Plymouth. In six pages, he described how I was to come to Crownhill, a suburb where he was staying with his elder brother, explaining I could stay the night and that he had bought a marvellous boat; also, perhaps I would help him in sailing it to Christchurch. I smelt trouble ahead, but decided to go anyway.

Packing a few things, I went by bus to Salisbury to catch the Atlantic Coast Express. The train was packed; well, all except one compartment – this contained the most ragged, rough-looking, bearded tramp that anyone could imagine. Wanting a seat and somewhere to dump my coat and case, I forced myself to join the wanderer.

He was smoking a short stumpy pipe and said, 'I'm glad you are smoking a pipe, too, it will keep the objectionable element out.'

My pipe nearly dropped from my mouth at this remark, but I soon settled down. After a few minutes, it struck me that I had seen this man before.

Meanwhile, he was gazing hard at me. Then at last he said, 'You are the fisher bloke who dug lugworm at Shell Bay, yes, you're him, eh?' Then he continued, 'Mind when I used to cadge a dozen worms?'

'That I do,' I answered.

He was none other than the Wild Man, who lived in Curlew Cottage, the man who used to walk out to the low-tide mark and use the umbrella frame to catch his fish. We talked of nothing but fishing until the train arrived at Yeovil. Here, a gypsy woman was looking for a seat. Seeing the old tramp and I chatting together on our own, she no doubt took us to be fellow travellers – in more ways than one – so into our compartment she came. Now I've never been averse to these sorts of people and have known many of the "Cooper, Lights and Sheens", and this old lady turned out to be one of the brighter lights – she would tell my fortune for a big piece of silver. More to pass the time than being a believer in luck, I gave her half a crown.

'Sir,' she began, 'you will face deadly peril at sea, but you will first go westwards on a journey with an old mate of yours, even as the moon moves over the seas I will, for another piece of silver …'

I laughed and ignored any prospects of further forecasts, yet I felt a bit uneasy at what she had predicted. Then, turning to the old tramp, she began to tell his future.

'You will again spend a winter near Penzance and your bank manager at Looe will have some very good news to tell you.'

'Good enough,' said the tramp, as he handed the gypsy a one-pound note.

I was frankly amazed, the woman had not even asked for reward. We drew into North Road and all alighted. So, bidding my two "companions" farewell, I took a taxi to Crownhill. Upon meeting Muggy, I could say little, as he was so busy talking about the wonderful boat he had bought.

At last, I broke in, 'Let's go down to the water and see her.'

'We can't. Matter o' fact, she's at Falmouth. We must go there first train tomorrow to fetch her and sail to Christchurch; do the trip in a day.'

'What,' I shouted, 'we got to go all the way down there? And sail nearly 200 miles in one day? You're mad.'

So, once again, I was involved in one of Muggy's escapades.

Well, the next day we arrived at Falmouth and found the chap who was selling the boat. He took us to the harbour, pointed out where the boat lay and then mysteriously disappeared, after receiving £28 from Muggy.

I could see that the boat was old and needed a lot of repairing, and said, 'Look at the gunwales, grooved by the ropes of thousands of lobster pots, she must be sixty years at least.'

I took some time going over every part of the hull and gear, and then went to a marine store for more rope, a set of pintles and two ringbolts – the rudder being insecure. We spent the rest of the day working on the boat. She had a clinker hull, mainmast, three sails and was some twenty feet in length with a six-foot beam. Upon pushing her into the water, we discovered several small leaks and I managed to get two dippers before the stores closed.

As darkness came down on us we went to a pub until closing time, and then returned to the boat and climbed in, intending to get some sleep. We nodded off for a minute or two, but got no real rest, due to the cold. As soon as it became light, we both set off for a run to try and get warm. But we had a third runner gaining on us, a policeman. He wanted to know why, when, where and what were the reasons for escape; not until he agreed to come back to the boat did he believe our explanations.

It was nearly noon by the time we had the boat ready and had obtained a supply of provisions, a hurricane lamp and other items, all of which I paid for, Muggy being almost broke through buying his boat.

Setting sail with a light westerly wind, we made slow progress. Every two hours it was necessary to bale out. At dusk, we had travelled perhaps thirty miles, at which point the wind began to freshen from the south-west and we surged ahead. By 2 a.m., we ought to have seen the Eddystone light or the lights of Plymouth, but saw none at all. As to what our position was we could not tell and a full gale was now raging.

Suddenly, we became broadside-on, the rudder pintles had come away from the transom and we were liable to capsize at any minute. It was not until I lowered the mainsail that a real danger was averted. Being adrift, not knowing how near we might be to a rocky coast, and in a boat that had begun to leak much faster (due to the pounding of the seas), made me think of the gypsy's warning – 'You will face deadly peril at sea ...'

'Muggy, we must drop the jib, pull the ballast astern and row, yes, row, to keep her before the seas.'

I had to shout this instruction because of the flapping canvas and howling wind in the rigging. With four oars between us, we kept the seas astern and so avoided capsizing. When daylight came, we saw the coast a few miles to port and as we coaxed the boat shorewards, I recognised that we were off Start Point.

Once under the lee of the coast, we got up sail and made for Dartmouth, as I knew one or two old mates who were among the old Towing and Salvage crew, and they lived near the river. On arrival, we got our boat ashore at a boatyard for an overhaul, found the transom to be rotten and had to have more timber added before it would take a new rudder, which had to be of a lighter weight. I managed to cash a cheque and paid up for the repairs. Had I foreseen the danger and cost of this trip, I would have heeded that gypsy's warning and pulled the communication cord there and then – it would have only cost me £5 at that point. As it was though, I was already nearly £29 out of pocket.

We still had much water to cover, so, setting sail again, we had the long, open run to Portland. This was uneventful, but took a whole day. We kept going throughout the night before a favourable westerly wind and at noon the following day, we were just off Southbourne, where the wind dropped. Here, we dropped anchor as a strong tide began to stop any progress. Moving off at 5 p.m., we reached Mudeford at 7.30 p.m. and finally arrived at Tuckton Bridge at about 9.15 p.m. I was back on *Thalassa* nigh midnight.

As I write this, I think back to some of those escapades with Muggy – Alan Mugford – can't forget 'em. At the moment, it is blowing a heavy gale outside, with heavy showers of rain, and I am seated by the fire. I recall the words the gypsy spoke once more. What did she know? I am still wondering to this day. My thoughts also go back to the tramp, once known as the Wild Man of the Heath. Yes, that night of the storm at Curlew Cottage, the old tramp's bed of heather upstairs and his heavy boots. Yet to think that he had made a fortune in his early life in Canada and that he'd lived among the Crees and could speak their tongue … he had finally revealed these facts as we reached North Road station that day. Where is he now? I wonder.

My overall expenses on that trip to Plymouth and Falmouth came to about £36, although I was never fully repaid by Muggy; I think I got about two-thirds of the money back. But it had been the same on all our other days (and nights) out; my hand always went deep into my pocket. This last venture, of course, occurred before he went away to Australia.

25

An Army of Crabs

One of my favourite fishing spots was just inside the harbour at Shell Bay, opposite Gravel Point. Here, three channels converged into one, forming a deep, narrow bottleneck. Any fish coming off the flats would eventually have to pass through this single, deep channel.

One day, I dug my usual 600 lugworms and then, at dead low water, rowed out to the lower end of this channel, anchored in two foot of water and awaited the flow of the incoming tide. It was too early to start fishing, so, for want of something to do, I peered into the clear water behind the stern. Almost the entire seabed was covered by millions of sand crabs, a huge army of them waiting for the tide to assist their advance. I learned something right at that moment – that it was hopeless to angle until the main body had spread over the mudflats. Curiosity made me drop over a two-hook baited line. Half a minute later, I pulled it up, only ten crabs on one hook and nine on the other, plus one trying to digest the lead.

I began to realise that once the tide was higher, this great army of sidesteppers would begin to disperse in battalions, then in companies, then into squads, only to spread out all over the mudflats and coastal shores. This is exactly what they do. So, if you had about 600 worms and continuously re-baited (after the main army has dispersed), you may actually catch a fish – or overbalance and be consumed. Yes, consumed by this vast army of returning, hungry crabs. They seem to be extremely fond of two-legged creatures. Anything edible, they eat. Dead bodies are high on their menu, so please yourself if you order a tin of the things.

Have I shocked my reader? Well, the edible kind of crab which is found in deeper water is more selective in its diet and is perhaps less inclined to eat the rubbish in inshore waters. Crabs are common on most of our coasts. I've fished at many resorts and they have eaten my bait; compared with every fish present, there are twenty hungry little crabs. So the odds are twenty to one against the fish.

I learned one or two lessons at the place I have described, Gravel Point. One was to fish the rising tide when it was over the banks, and another thing was to start at the top of the tide and spend two hours at the bottleneck. My usual catch was something between thirty and forty flatfish, one or two silver eels and the odd bass.

One afternoon, I landed on Brownsea Island to collect some clean sand for keeping worm supplies in. Nearby was a large pool of water, left by a high tide, where I noticed a shoal of small fish, so I waded in after them. They dashed into a mass of flannel weed from which they could not escape, and became entangled in it. I picked up over 400 pilchards that rarely came farther east than Plymouth. On my way back to *Thalassa*, I had an hour's bass fishing and got about 17 lb, best one nearly 8 lb.

I was doing very well selling bait at the time. I could clear everything that my nine men could obtain. Even my wife sometimes dug up some 600 worms when the demand was heavy.

But by May 1939, trade began to fall off. There was not as much demand for my boats, either. War clouds were gathering, things got worse and I had to discharge my diggers. Then, in August, war was declared. Restrictions came in regarding the movements of all craft, but I registered Tam and had a permit to use her, but only during daylight hours. This handicap prevented me from going on my long day trips, which often took twelve hours.

Raiders began to drop bombs in October in our area, so I sent my wife to her mother's home. One bomb hit the sea wall seventy yards away, causing some of our windows to blow outwards; a blast often does this. Only near hits make windows and doors blow inwards.

Soon, I had to sell *Thalassa* for a mere song, though I didn't feel like singing. I also sold my other boats for very poor sums, but Tam went into storage. She had been in constant use for nearly twenty years and I could not bring myself to sell her. In all my miles on the open sea, in all weathers, we had never come to grief and she was still in good condition. Before storing her, I gave her a coat of paint; blue top sides,

a two-inch white line just below the gunwales and a French grey hull –
my entire little fleet had similar colours.

I still continued doing various sorts of marine jobs round the
harbour, cycling from the village which lay three miles north of Poole,
where I had now gone to live, though we even had the bombs out there.
Late one night, I could hear a plane, but as I was about to open the
door, a bomb was dropped, taking the door out of my hand. Another
time, two landmines dropped on a farmhouse – never did find any trace
of the family.

I became an air-raid warden during the war, which meant taking a
turn on night duty and missing much sleep, also having to work as
normal the following day. No matter how long the alert lasted, we had
to be on patrol. The alerts often lasted ten or eleven hours, because the
raids extended to the Midlands and the North, with the planes passing
over our district both when coming and going.

We did not get many bombs, but on one particular night, when I was
out at about 1.15 a.m., a plane began to circle low overhead. Soon, I
heard the whistle of descending bombs, so lay down, only to hear two
bangs – seemed as if the path lifted up, yet they fell 200 yards away. It
gave me a scare, not half. It is thought that many of the bombs which
fell on the mudbanks in Poole Harbour never exploded. Instead, they
penetrated deep into soft mire.

In May 1940, hundreds of French and Belgian fishing boats arrived
loaded with refugees. The harbour was very busy with our flying boats
and coastal shipping at the time and a couple of Dutch traders were
blown up by magnetic mines near to the bar, which is three miles beyond
the harbour mouth. Nothing of over four feet in length remained of
these two ships. I went out to the spot, but all I could find was a set of
code flags, a first-aid chest and bits of hatch covers.

It was a great mystery as to how the German seaplane managed to
place six magnetic mines in the narrow cut, which had been dredged in
the bar, on such a dark night. The pilot of the plane must have been as
familiar with the actual position of the cut as any of our seagoing folk.
To make certain that the channel was clear of further mines, a wooden-
hulled tug towed metal barges to and fro, using a two-rope of about 400
yards in length. Four metal barges were lost in the process, but it

destroyed the remaining mines. Later, by some special means of insulation, they made the vessels impervious to the magnetic influence of this type of mine. All ships with this protection henceforth had a yellow band printed around their hulls.

26

Inland to the River

Due to the war, I became totally unemployed, what with no longer having our floating home and very few people being around who wanted to buy bait. Mind, there were jobs galore of the routine sort, indoors. But after a life of freedom, such employment could not and would not blend with my nature. I scanned the "situations vacant" column for weeks, for months, but without result. With having so much spare time, I went back to beachcombing. Some days I got a pocketful of silver, other days mostly coppers.

By the end of 1941, I was getting desperate, and so was my wife. We were down to our last few pounds. Then, one morning, I saw something in the *Western Gazette*: river keeper wanted on the Dorset Stour, apply to Secretary, Ferndown Golf Club. Surely there would be a crowd of chaps after the job, I thought. Then I thought again – no, perhaps not. So many were involved now with war work. I wonder what part of this sixty-five-mile Stour it might be.

Setting off on my bike, I covered the seven miles to Ferndown faster than I have ever ridden before. Reaching the golf club, I rushed into the office without even knocking first on the door. Seated at his desk was Mr Beard, `the secretary. Before he could reprimand me for my sudden intrusion, I said, 'I've come for the job.'

Seeing I was somewhat exhausted after my furious ride, he poured out a whisky and then asked, 'But won't you be liable for work of national importance?'

I answered, 'No, I'm an air-raid warden.'

Then he went on, 'The water is at Throop, probably you do not know of it.'

I almost whispered, 'What I did see of the water is by now in the sea, see?'

I then told him of my early years there and about how I had got to know the salmon anglers, etc. Then he said, 'Come into the lounge and meet some of the new fishing syndicate.'

I was then introduced to some of the members. They seemed to be surprised and pleased that they had found a man who actually knew the Throop waters. I told them several "fishy" tales, which went down well, and so did the whisky. In fact, they appeared very surprised as to how rapidly each bottle became empty.

Much refreshed in mind, "spirit", and body, I mounted my bike at the fourth attempt and made for Throop to see my new home. It was a cottage along the road towards Holdenhurst and on the Earl of Malmesbury's estate, and we moved in at the end of the month, four weeks before the salmon season commenced. This gave me time to put some of the banks and footbridges in order, and to hire a lorry to bring two of my boats over from Sandbanks.

We were limited to twelve rods; each could fish on any two days each week. Most of the other members had no idea about salmon fishing and this meant I had to be in almost constant attendance. The first fish was taken by Dr Moore on 9 February, a fine specimen of 25 lb. As each fish was caught, I had to ring all the other members.

They would want to know who caught it, and where, also what lure was used, and other details; this would mean that I would be sat at my telephone for the best part of two hours in the evening "telling the tale" and giving advice, often finding numbers engaged and then having to ring a second time.

Some of my gents simply couldn't catch a fish. After wasting a few weeks, they would come to me and say, 'Perhaps you could get me a salmon, I'll make it worth your while.'

On another such occasion, a member was unwell and rang to ask me to fish for him. Now at that time I only had a cheap boy's roach rod; however, I set off up to James' Pool and was into a fish on my third cast. I had been playing it for about ten minutes when the rod broke off short, near the butt, the upper two sections going down onto the salmon's nose. Now I was very keen to get this fish on the bank for this nice old gent, but I was severely handicapped with only twenty inches of rod in my hands. However, I succeeded at last – weight twenty-four and a half pounds.

I recall another morning when a mad-brained golfer phoned, saying, 'Go straight to the mill, take my rod, it is now eleven, will come on next bus, get me a salmon without delay.'

Now he had already been to the river three times before for spells of only thirty minutes each time. On each occasion, he had thrown his rod onto the ground remarking, 'There's no fish here,' and hastened away. So, leaving home at 11.10 a.m. or thereabouts, I reached the river at 11.20 a.m., hooked a fish at 11.25 a.m. and landed it at 11.40 a.m. – eighteen and a half pound.

He arrived at 11.50 a.m., never so much as attempted to angle, gave me a bottle of gin and departed. Not liking gin, I sold it for a pound. I found out later that he had told the club he had caught it.

Another time, I had an old gent with me and at about noon, he said, 'I'm a bit tired, here, have a go.'

Changing his lure for a favourite one of my own, I was into a fish on my second cast. After playing it for a few minutes, I passed the rod back to the gent and soon gaffed a twenty-one-pounder. I shall have more to say about getting fish for rods later on.

A certain Wednesday stays in my mind, when it blew a gale and rained throughout the day. I got pretty wet in the morning when out with two gents, and was out again in the afternoon with four more.

One of these was a Mr Basset. In casting, the wind took his fly over to the far bank and it caught fast on a high rock. To release it, I had to go half a mile up river in order to cross at the weir. Reaching the rock, I got out to the fly, freed it and threw it into the river, where a salmon almost took it out of my hand – before the gent could start to reel in he was into the fish. I was so amazed that I nearly slipped off of the rocky ledge.

Getting to the bank, I ran all the way back to be ready to use my gaff. But there were three more fellows, each with a gaff, standing in a row. Feeling superfluous, I stood back. All at once, the fish came close in. Three gaffs went into the water, they all missed. In the confusion, I poked my gaff between Lord Lytton's legs. As I pulled the fish between the said Lordship's legs, it caused him to sit down in the river. But everyone was elated to see a 20 lb salmon safely on the bank. I was especially happy, knowing that this fish had almost taken the Blue Charm out of my hand.

A particularly lucky afternoon in June comes to mind, when the fish are usually difficult to lure in, because of the high water temperature. Taking a boat, I rowed up river a couple of miles, intending to cut some sedge, but as I neared Elliot's Pool, a large fish surfaced. Having my tackle on board at the time, I made a few casts and must have hooked the fish that had shown. Within a few minutes, I landed it, 29 lb. Continuing on to James' Pool, something made me try a few casts here, too. Soon, another fish was hooked. This proved to be heavier still, 32 lb.

That same season, I got two of 28 lb each. It was rather odd how I managed to hook one of these fish at dusk in the Nettle Field though. Starting to cast at the lower end, I fished the Saucer Pool, which was a small, round hollow of some five yards in diameter. Soon, I was into a fish. It dashed downstream for about forty yards, before getting behind a tree, which had trailing branches in the river, my line among them. The only thing we could do was to wait, leaving the line slack. After what seemed ages, the fish moved across river, freeing the line of the branches. Still leaving my line slack, the fish made its way upstream for 200 yards. Here, I played it, determined that it would not get back to the tree below – it nearly did, once – but at last I got it out, almost in total darkness.

The next day, I had to send this salmon to London by passenger train. It took me two hours to make a box for it, four feet by one foot by ten inches, and then I had to push it the two miles to Boscombe Station on my bike, before sending a telegram ahead for the gent to meet the train.

27

Poachers Galore

Throop Fishery might almost be said to be at the "back door of Bournemouth". By this, I mean that it is only two miles from a population of over 80,000, so I was bothered by many people who had been coming to the riverside, for bathing, poaching and picnicking. For several years, no keepers had been employed. Things had got so bad that in my first year on the job, I had to take offenders to court on eight separate occasions. Usually, I would give a poacher a warning and send them away. Only if I caught them a second time, or if it was a serious matter, did I take proceedings.

One evening, I was sat by the fire when the phone rang.

'Is that you?' a voice asked.

'Yes, what is it?' I enquired.

'It's me, Mr Harris, you know me. Well, I was passing along the road by the mill about three or thereabouts, when I heard a loud bang. Then I saw two soldiers at the weir pool, one of them dived into the water and got hold of a big fish of some sort.'

After asking him a few more questions, I went to the weir pool with a torch and found a number of dead fish, including two large salmon. A label lay nearby; on it in red letters was: "Handle with care, keep dry, dangerous." Glancing at my watch, I noticed that it was 8.45 p.m. Without wasting any further time, I went and fetched our local policeman. He made a few notes and agreed to make enquiries early the following day. No more could be done that night, so I went home and thought the matter over most carefully.

I recalled seeing two soldiers near the pool a week previously. I was near them when one of the men asked a salmon angler about the salmon ladder. I remembered that both of the men had been wearing green berets, one of them was tall and thin, the other was shorter and thickset.

The next morning, I phoned Mr Harris, but he could not add more to what he had first told me and nor did he recall the colour of their hats, all he could say was that it was a bitterly cold day to choose to dive into an icy-cold river. With very little evidence and our policeman being engaged on another matter, I decided to go to the commanding officer of the Fifth Commandos, who were billeted in hotels on the Boscombe Cliffs, and see if I could identify the men in question.

Closely, I looked at every soldier and, sure enough, I recognised the two I had seen at the weir. At first, they denied going to the river, but when I said I could call further witnesses, they owned up. Incidentally, it was true as regards to other witnesses; some children near our village had seen two soldiers pushing a bike that had two sacks of big fish. They admitted to using a fuse and detonator and to taking away five salmon averaging 20 lb, also to selling the fish to a dealer.

I recovered the salmon, putting them in cold storage until the case came up. Both fellows were found guilty, but were let off lightly having been on active service. Each was fined five guineas, plus 2 guineas in costs, and the dealer was fined fifteen guineas. The actual loss of fish life can only be guessed at; I also recovered two more salmon and about 300 coarse fish.

My next case was a most unusual kind, as it concerned a policeman and it did not come to my notice until four months after the offence had taken place.

I was having a drink one morning and there was a group of men chatting and passing round some photos, when one said to another, 'Whopper, wer' did Marley catch it eh, an' I wonder 'ow?'

'Oh, he caught it below Moor's Island, Throop Water, 'bout four or five months ago. Said it was 22 lb, and he sold it to a fish shop for £4 2s 6d.'

This was startling news of which I had heard nothing until this moment, and then only by chance. Now, whoever this man Marley was, he certainly was not one of my syndicate members, although he could have been on our water with a 2s 6d ticket for coarse fishing; we had recently started these day tickets, hoping it would reduce poaching.

I butted in, saying, 'Excuse me, I couldn't help seeing the photo of that fine salmon, wonder who developed it?'

It was a chance shot, but it worked, and one of the fellows said, 'Was developed down Pokesdown Hill, next to Jean's shoe shop.'

Without undue haste, I left the inn and walked down the hill, until I came to a chemist adjoining the shoe shop.

Entering, I casually bought a toothbrush and then, in an offhand sort of way, asked, 'You don't happen to have any pictures of fish by any chance? I collect them.'

'Oh, I got one or two. Wait a minute, I'll have a look.'

Soon, he handed me several, yes, one of a tall fellow with a big salmon.

'I shall have to ask you to lend me this snap, or, better still, supply me with a copy. I believe this concerns a Mr Marley?'

'Why, what's the matter, nothing amiss, I hope?'

'Only that there may be need for you to go to court to say that you actually saw this fish visually and also took the photo.'

At first, the chemist did not seem to want to cooperate, but after I had explained that he would be compensated if he attended court as a witness, he became more at ease. I then contacted two more fellows to whom Marley had said that he had caught the salmon, one being the fishmonger who had bought the fish.

Finally, I found Marley, and this is what he told me: 'I went to the lower end of Moor's Island for some roach. A large salmon drifted close into the bank. It was dead, but appeared to be in quite good condition, so I took it on and flogged it.'

When the case camp up, it came to light that the constable had told two different tales, one that he had caught the fish, the other that he had found it dead. This was confirmed by the witnesses. Now it is just as illegal to take a dead salmon as it is to take a live one, being a game fish. He was, therefore, found guilty, but we did not press the case, we left it for the superintendent to deal with the constable. I heard later that the fellow had been transferred to another town, where there was no river.

One August evening, I was about to go home when a man turned up, saying, 'It's too late to justify me paying for a day ticket, I only want to fish for an hour anyway, and besides I got no bait.'

Now he was a well-known poacher, as I well knew, yet I could hardly ask for half a crown at that time of the evening, so I said, 'But what about bait?'

'Give me an hour and you'll see,' he added.

I agreed to this, provided I could be present. First, he baited his rod with a dewberry and caught a chub. Then he found a black-and-gold caterpillar and caught a roach. Next, he obtained an oval, flat seed from a tall plant and with this, he soon had a dace. Finally, he found a grub in the roots of a dock and with this, he took his fourth fish, a perch of one and a half pounds. Frankly, I was amazed. All done in fifty minutes. I felt that I owed him something for the exhibition.

I heard later that he had gone to Longham shortly after and he'd caught four salmon, all out of the same pool. Two of my rods had fished that pool the previous day and caught nothing. What makes it more surprising though, is that those four salmon were taken on orange peel, spun on a treble mount.

Some weeks later, he came to the mill one day at midday with his rod and a can containing nineteen live bait. He said, 'Shan't want a ticket, I'm going over to the Moor's River.'

At about 7 p.m., he came back with nineteen pike in a large sack, as much as he could carry, all caught on these nineteen live baits. A most remarkable feat.

28

Opposite Bank

At the upper end of our water we did not have the rights on both banks. For about a mile, we only had the left-hand bank. This rather annoyed me, as poachers on the other side were beyond my authority – at least they were at that time. I would see these fellows taking fish with impunity.

Going to the top water one evening, I saw the poacher who had caught the four fish without using normal baits. With him was his father, who was also a well-known poacher. I called to him across the water and asked what he had done with the nineteen pike.

He replied, 'Took 'em to the fish shop near Wooten Gardens where a lot of Jews live. Got £3 10s for 'em. Nearly got as many today between us, also a trout, a good 5 lb.'

He pulled a sack from the undergrowth and held it up, crammed full of fish, yet I could do nothing about it, as the owner of the fishing rights never stopped anyone from fishing there. I was, of course, aware that neither of these men had a game licence to cover trout or an annual rod licence of two shillings and sixpence, which had recently become law for anyone wishing to fish anywhere for coarse fish.

Another spot of bother I had was with two boys who made use of a boat which I kept on this upper stretch. They used it to rob the water birds' nests. I caught them on the job one day, when I found a sock on the bank full of moorhens' eggs. I picked it up and gave them a few whacks across their backsides, eggsactly what they deserved. They never came back.

I had to report two lads one Sunday. It was pouring with rain and I was standing under a shelter near the road. I could see these two lads in a boat, about 200 yards downriver, that belonged to the Catchment Board. Despite the rain, one of them appeared to be sawing something, while the other lad was ripping planks from the floorboards. Then, suddenly, the boat started to drift away in the fast flowing water. Alarmed, they scrambled ashore.

I stopped them as they came round the back of the mill and took their names and addresses, later reporting the affair to the offices of the Board, who took proceedings and were awarded £4 in damages.

The boat was recovered two miles downstream. The mooring chain had been cut with a hacksaw and the floorboards were all broken up and some parts missing. The lads intended using the loosened planks as paddles, but panicked when they got caught in a fast current.

I was at the mill one Easter, when five boats came drifting down. A couple of these jammed in the hatches and were crushed to pieces, but we managed to pull the other three ashore. Later that day, I found two more boats, which had drifted into a bed of reeds; boys had set all these craft adrift from near Longham.

During the coarse-fishing season, I would be at the mill on Sundays from 1.30 p.m. onwards. This was the only place where one could cross the river and with it being near to the road, most anglers came here. Each man would ask for a ticket and tender a pound note. Soon, I would have no change left and would say, 'Here is your ticket, pay on return'. Did they come back? No. Some of them dodged out another way and I had to make good the half-crowns to comply with the counterfoils in the ticket book. One Sunday, I was seventeen shillings and sixpence out of pocket. On £3 a week wages, it was no joke, however, I did begin to make a bit by letting out my boats. Also, during the actual salmon season, the tips helped.

My wife assisted me by selling tickets at the door, asking anglers in when the weather worsened, making tea, storing their gear, telling them how to reach certain areas or where to park their cars, and a whole host of other things, so we were both occupied. Also, records had to be kept, takings checked and the phone was often in use; never in my life has there been a dull moment. Seldom did I eat a meal without some sort of interruption. I had just sat down for dinner one day, when a lad rushed in to say that he had caught a salmon and would I come down to the river? He had no right to take a salmon.

'Where is it?' I asked.

'I got it in my keepnet, what must I do with it?'

We set off to the field, a mile away downriver. Reaching the spot where the boy had been fishing, I lifted the keepnet out of the river. Inside it was one of the biggest chub I had ever seen. Perhaps it was not surprising that the boy had thought it to be a salmon. My pocket spring balance registered nearly 17 lb.

'Worth a newspaper prize,' I remarked.

'No, I'm not keen to enter for that, let's put it back, it's no good for eating, quite thought I'd landed a salmon though,' he said.

I returned to my dinner, long-since cold.

Just a week later, I was again called from the table. A neighbour rushed in, saying, in one breath, 'Oh, what shall I do? I've left me saucepan on; 'twill boil over and put out the gas, and I forgot to shut me door, so fowls will be in at the pastry. I'm expecting me sister who is expecting and there is a fisherman down in Bligden's field and he be up in a tree and a bull is a waiting for him to come down. Oh, what's to be done?'

Now we river keepers get some funny jobs, but this was a new one on me. Anyhow, I had to do something, so, getting up from my dinner, I thanked the woman for her explicit and detailed explanation, went out into the garden, picked up six turnips, placed them in my pockets and then, with some trepidation, proceeded towards the scene. Sure enough, there was my tall and hefty angler halfway up one of the willows; below was the bull, just about to finish chewing up an expensive pair of gauntlets. As I warily approached the animal, I realised who it belonged to. Now, less warily, I walked towards it more bravely and on reaching it, I gave it one of the turnips. The bull eagerly accepted it, so I began to walk into the field with a second turnip in my hand and the bull followed. Eventually, I reached the centre of the field with only one turnip left. Every twenty yards, I had enticed the animal with a turnip. Then I called to the angler to climb down and run for the gate at the lane – well, never before had I seen anyone run like he did.

Me? Oh, very casually, I strolled slowly towards the gate, climbed over and said, 'Sorry about the gloves; seems to have an appetite.'

He was still gasping for breath and between each gasp, he managed to say, 'You ... are ... a hero.'

'Rubbish,' I replied, in an offhand sort of way, 'that bull could not have hurt anybody; there was about seven foot of chain hanging from its neck. I knew better than to attempt to run, because if it trod on the chain it would stumble and fall. The bull had been tethered to a post and the chain had broken at a weak spot.'

But the fellow would insist on my accepting ten shillings – to which I muttered a faint "no" just once. Then I took him to another meadow, where he got an 8 lb pike on second cast and I went home to a belated dinner.

Having been talking about the lordly salmon, let's say something about how we catch them – fifty per cent are all down to luck, the other fifty per cent by skill and ability. But the man who gets 100 per cent is the one who makes a habit of deep attention to detail; he will get to know just why his quarry is to be located in only certain straight glides. He will know that he has to put his lure in front of the fish, not just once, but perhaps twice or even six times. Seldom does a fish take hold at the first offer, yet we read in most books and articles to "cast once every yard as we go along". No wonder some anglers are misinformed, this method means that if the fish fails to take at the first offer, then the second cast comes back near its tail.

It may sound strange, but if you should catch a fish at a recognised spot, another fish will be sure to take up the same position, so that is why it is important that you note some mark on the bank, just where a fish takes the lure. It is important to know this to within twelve inches, because it may well mean that you can go back to that precise spot the next day and take another fish.

My success is well known among anglers. My average time to hook a fish is in less than six minutes. I do not waste all day flogging the water, I concentrate on small details. Many fish I've had within three minutes, two under five seconds, and most of these have been caught "to order", and, generally, my fishing time has been from 7.30 a.m. to 8.00 a.m. with a half-hour at sunset.

Fishing the whole length of a pool is time wasted, your fish will be in the neck or tail of a pool; they only go into the pool if alarmed. My best three fish were thirty-seven, thirty-seven and thirty-six and a half pounds. During my best season, my average fish weighed 22 lb.

The Stour spreads very wide at times of flooding. At Throop, it covers the meadows to a width of nearly one and a half miles. We had such a flood once resulting in four of our horses being marooned. They were on a small area that was fast becoming covered with water and they were in a state of near-panic. I had to take the boat and go out to them, and then catch one at a time and entice it to swim after the boat, having attached one end of the rope to the animal's neck and the other end of the rope to my stern. The fourth horse nearly finished us both off. In crossing the main river – here, the current was very fast – the animal was being carried down towards the hatches. It was a miracle how we managed to get clear of the flow; the whole job took four hours and nothing for it.

But river keepers do lots of jobs that they never get paid for, such as putting out fires, burying drowned animals, rounding up stray cattle, removing broken bottles and tins, securing gates, etc. Cows fall in sometimes, when drinking, so I always carried a spade and a thick length of rope in the boat. By digging a "step" on the bank and getting my rope round the cow's neck behind its horns, I would get it to the bank and entice it to get its two forefeet on to the step. Then, by pulling on the rope, the animal could scramble out of the water.

29

Fantastic, Yet True

Before I came back to the Dorset Stour as keeper, only season tickets had been available, so poaching had been rife. The introduction of day tickets overcame much of this trouble; also, I took on the extra job of area water-bailiff for the old Board of Conservators. This was really an honorary post, being unpaid, except for the sum of £15 annually to cover cycle maintenance, lunches away from home, postage, etc. I had about sixteen miles of the riverbank to visit once weekly and my work entailed issuing licences, reporting pollution and reducing poaching.

More and more anglers were coming to my own five miles of water, so I was kept busy every day, especially on Sundays. During the evenings, too, there was always much to do; repairing tackle, accounts and records to keep up to date and callers, in addition to answering the telephone. No wonder angling is the finest sport and pastime in the world. Mind, some happenings can be sad ones.

One cold, March evening there was a heavy knocking on my door. Before I could open it, a salmon angler barged in. He was in a most furious state of mind, cursing everybody who had ever walked a riverbank. Due to the flow of adjectives, I cannot repeat what he had to say. But, that afternoon, he had gone to Bosley pool to try and fish for a salmon, which in itself was not too hopeful, as the run of fish was late that year, with only three, so far, having been taken. When it was nearly dark, he had hooked a heavy fish, which put up a terrific fight. It tore round and round the pool. Two fellows came along on the opposite side of the bank and stood watching. They just stood there, saying not a word. Then, ten minutes later, the salmon did a much wider circle round the pool, passing close to the angler, but he missed driving in the gaff. It then went round the far side of the pool. As it did so, one of the

119

fellows stepped into the water, got hold of the salmon and clambered up the bank; the other man then cut the line and they vanished into the darkening night. No wonder the angler was distraught to lose such a big fish like that, they being few and hard to come by.

'Can you trace these rogues?' he asked.

'You say it was too dark to recognise them again; besides, we have not got the fishing rights on the opposite bank,' I replied.

The next incident happened at Withy Pool No. 2 one afternoon in July, when the river was low and clear. One of the salmon anglers turned up, but, thinking that conditions looked hopeless, he decided to have a go for one of the large chub in the pool instead, so I mixed up some bread paste with a few drops of pilchard oil and baited his No. 6 hook, with a breaking strain of only 4 lb.

Now I knew there were three or four salmon in this pool, and one of these came and took the hook. What a commotion, the angler dare not put on too much pressure; the only thing for it was to tire the fish slowly, even if it took a couple of hours or more. After almost three hours, the fish came close under our bank, but I was unable to reach it due to the water being so low and the bank high. Racing back to the mill, I returned with my long boathook, to which I fixed my gaff with two lashings of weak Black Spider line. When the fish again came near, I managed to reach it. But the weight of the salmon as I lifted it clear of the water caused both lashings to break. It fell back into the water, taking my gaff with it.

What a way to lose our prize; we were both speechless for a few moments, and then came lamentations. But what about my treasured gaff that had lifted out hundreds of salmon? Still holding the boathook, I could see the handle of my gaff and I managed to hook it out, nearly falling in whilst doing so. For some while, we sat on the bank – any further fishing was farthest from our minds.

We had just decided to pack up, when something caught my eye about 40 yards downstream. It was a big salmon rolling over and over in a fast flow that passed a small island of gravel. Picking up my gaff, I ran along the bank. Jumping into the water, I reached the gravel just as the fish was about to drift into a deep pool. With the fish on my gaff, I struggled back to land with the twenty-four-pounder.

The reason why the salmon was drifting broadside was due to when I had first driven the gaff in. I had severed the vertebrae of its spine, so it could not use its tail, thus rendering it like a ship without a rudder. Had I been one second later, I would never have reached it, so it was a happy ending after all.

My next incident is about a colonel who came to the river the day before the season opened – just to try out his tackle to make sure everything was in working order. Yes, everything was in working order. By accident (or perhaps it was design), he caught a 25 lb salmon. What a tragedy to have to put it back – the very idea of it. So he went to a cottager and borrowed a sack. Placing the fish in it, he secured the sack to the roots of a willow tree that was growing out of the bank, intending on returning in the morning when the season would be legally open and "catch it again", as you might say. But the cottager in question was a curious fellow. He knew the season had not yet commenced, so he had watched the colonel from a back window.

That same evening, all the villagers had a cutlet of very fresh salmon for dinner. As to what the colonel had to say about it when he returned the following morning, that will never be known.

A certain Lord Strabolgi fished my waters several seasons. During his naval career, he was known as Commander Kenworthy. I was always glad to see him, always a £1 tip, always £5 if he caught a salmon, always a full flask to start the day.

One morning, he hooked a fish at No. 1 Withy Pool. A narrow stream entered the top of this pool, which was no more than two feet in depth and three feet wide. This particular salmon left the river and went 200 yards up this stream, with his Lordship following. I could have gaffed it on a score of occasions, but he preferred not and it was coaxed back to the river. What a dance that fish led us. Finally, I got it out 400 yards down river, 18 lb.

He had started to fish one morning when a telegram came to say that he was wanted back at the house. Before he dashed off, he said, 'Catch me a fish, I will send a taxi for it to be taken to my Bournemouth hotel. Will be back tomorrow.'

Some of my best anglers have been the weaker (?) sex.

Lady M came over one day with her maid and I rowed them up river.

The day was very hot and conditions seemed hopeless. Anyway, she caught a nice fish before noon, and then after lunch she had a nap in the field, her rod at the stern of the boat. Having nothing better to do, I picked up the rod and made a short cast. A fish took at once, so I called to the maid to go and awaken her Ladyship.

Passing her the rod, I said, 'It's all yours.'

She let that fish do just what it liked, hardly putting on any pressure, playing it from one position for a full eighty minutes. I said nothing, as long as my angler does nothing seriously wrong I do not interfere. At last, the salmon began to tire and I pulled it out, 21 lb.

'Both fish took some time,' I casually remarked, 'but you certainly handled them very well.'

Her Ladyship replied, 'You see, my line was perished; it had been in use for seven years in Vancouver, they sent me over the wrong reel. When I tested the line this morning, it parted at two-pound strain. Not really expecting to catch salmon, I did not bother to get a new line.'

Young Know-alls

There is more to tell about lady anglers, but we shall come to that presently, as right at this moment, I am annoyed, perturbed and disgusted with some of the younger writers of today.

Back between 1906 and 1926, the angling journals contained articles of general interest, which told of interesting incidents by river, lake and sea, amusing happenings and so on. Since about 1926, we have had an ever-increasing number of young writers, all trying to tell us how to catch fish. I know two lads, one of whom is only seventeen, who get most of their ideas from books, having been in their dens and read about a hundred books on our sport. Neither of these lads fishes more than once a month, and then only on one or two different waters.

In recent years, we have had so much bickering, backbiting and repetition, so there has been much theory and dogmatic, meaningless jumble. I can positively swear that I had read not less than 5,191 times that roach take maggots, chub take cheese and bass take sand eel. For each of these three species we are told just how we are to proceed to catch them. But these young writers fail to realise that time of year, the condition of the water and locality, all call for the angler to use his own common sense, to experiment, to speculate, to rely on his own initiative.

I have realised that after many long days by the waterside, I know very little. Yet these younger writers seem to know so much. If they really do, then why don't they catch more and better fish? They have even formed Specimen Hunter Groups, but how rarely do they land a so-called specimen? It is the boys with second-rate tackle who continually get the big fish, the said angling paper proves this to be a fact. But I am thankful that I have not read books on angling. I've had to learn the hard way, the best way. I have been lucky in that I've been by the water all my life, apart from three years at school and war service and even then, I was fishing at every opportunity. My final total of fish landed by hook amounts to more than 1,300,000, and most of those have been caught on crude, cheap tackle.

Many a time it has been suggested that I write a book on how to catch fish, but why should I add to the overloaded bookshelves with yet another discourse on this subject? True, I could write a book on catching salmon, but why should I give away certain secrets? True, I've specialised in my methods, whereby I average less than six minutes in getting my fish to take my lure, and about eight minutes in playing it – perhaps I developed a sixth sense in getting my salmon so often, I don't know. If I put all the details in print, it would all be copied in other books. If my methods were adopted, it might well mean that salmon would be caught too easily and then they would become extinct.

My salmon fishing has only been done on the Avon, Stour, Frome, Taw and Test. None of these rivers have a big run of fish and I had to limit myself in latter years to only angling in April and May. Years back, I used to fish in February and March, avoiding kelt by using a thick-bodied lure. This, they would not take because, due to throat contraction, they are unable to accept such a lure. Since then, I've given up fishing in June, as most of the fish are getting out of condition. I prefer to spend hours just watching them, sending them signals with my arms, making them turn left or rise to the surface and other tricks.

It was amusing to lower some bait into the water without any hooks, and watch just how a salmon behaves, how it accepts it and the way in which it takes hold. It was due to these tests that I found that (in most instances) a fish ignores your offer first time, moves slightly at the second offer, the third time it nearly takes it and the fourth time it grabs it.

I'm told that the book says "Make a cast every yard as you walk along". No wonder few fish are caught. You first have to know exactly where your fish lies to within a foot. But before you know just where each fish lies, you must know the nature of the river bed, the actual straight flow, the depth and other things. All of these would take too long to explain here. Perhaps it all boils down to that sixth sense, if you can come by it. There is much more in this than any words of mine can express.

I have lived a "wild life" with nature, and thus I know some secrets of the wilds: to make a 2 lb roach accept my bait, to compel a sleepy pike to grab my wagtail, to interest a plaice or dab when I wanted to catch them.

Anglers who take a dozen loaves to use as ground bait should know better. I have taken many thousands of fish without it. When you think of the millions of starving people around the world, you know that it is the wrong thing to do. The angler is getting caught by the glittering things in the tackle shops, the gadgets. They are being overloaded with masses of equipment that they have no need of. For example, look at the hundreds of spinning lures made to lose fish.

No hard lure is advisable. In seven times out of ten, if a fish feels the metal or wooden lure, it lets go. Devons are the worst of all. I know fish are caught on these, simply because there are thousands being used every day, but if soft spinners such as wagtails and rubber ones were in use more often, then fish would be hooked more often and more securely. One treble hook is enough; more than one treble means that your spinner rotates at reduced speed, due to water friction. A spinning lure must rotate rapidly and smoothly, even in static water, in order for it to interest a fish.

There are three kinds of river fish that I gave up catching a long time ago – carp and tench, because they are ugly brutes, and bream, because they are slimy things and give themselves up. How a fellow can catch a net full of these fish I cannot understand, a bream of 6 to 10 lb is well worth taking, but fifty of 3 lb each must be a monotonous business. Sea bream is a different thing though, as it is a sporting fish and excellent for the table.

At one time, the Dorset Stour held many pike of all sizes. I recall a huge one, which the estate workers trapped in a ditch once; they heaved it ashore with their spades, and it weighed in at 46 lb. Two others, taken on the rod near Stuart's Oak, were 41½ lb and 41 lb. Mr Keen, the Thames professional, brought a client to my water for a day's pike fishing once and with eighty live baits, they took nearly three and a half hundredweight.

The increasing numbers of salmon anglers have thinned out the pike these days and the few that remain are caught before they can grow to any size. I remember taking old Tom Smith, the farmer, up river for the pike once, as we still had a fair number near the Reed Island. He fished all day, and never so much as a bite.

At dusk, he said, 'It's no good; chuck the last of that live bait in, best pack up.'

As I threw the last little fish back into the water, a huge pike came out from under our bank and took it.

'There, Pond, what do you think of that?'

Words failed me. Poor old Tom, but that's the luck of the game.

Mr C. Hunt came out with me one morning and at lunchtime, he said, 'I shall rest for a while; come back about 2.45 p.m.'

So I returned, but could not find any trace of him. After a while, I heard some pigs grunting in an orchard. Curious to know why they were so noisy, I went to find out. Mr Hunt was sound asleep at the base of an apple tree, snoring loudly, and surrounded by a circle of porkers, who were grunting in sympathy.

30

Creating a Disturbance

I came to know a certain well-known gentleman of Christchurch, who was a justice of the peace, through being made Hon. Bailiff. He had a yacht in the tidal part of the Stour and one very hot afternoon, he decided to go for a sail. But, alas, the wind fell, so he went into the cabin and drifted off to sleep.

But not for long. Suddenly, he was awakened by strange noises. It sounded as if someone was bashing the garden shed to pieces, but this wasn't the garden. Now thoroughly alarmed, he crawled into the cockpit and looked over the transom. There, in his dinghy, was a huge salmon. The fish had been jumping and it had accidentally landed in the little boat, but the three seats had prevented it from leaping back into the water. Its desperate struggles were the cause of all the noise.

Talk about creating a disturbance, had he not had just such a case at court that very morning? Due to its frantic struggles and the hot sun, the fish soon expired. So the respected JP rowed ashore and proceeded up the high street with the salmon. I happened to meet him, so I asked how he came by the fish, as I knew that he had no licence. Surely here was a case of breaking the fishery law. But I could do nothing about it; I could not charge him, because the salmon had not been caught, illegally purchased, netted or procured by otherwise devious means; the fish had given itself up. Nothing in legal phraseology could prove him guilty.

There was one day though, when I was the guilty one. Having a day off from the river, I went boat fishing at Boscombe. On the way home, I went into a greengrocer's shop and asked him to weigh my catch, which came to 22 lb. My left knee touched a tray of apples, and five rolled into my wellington boot. Being in a hurry to catch the next bus,

I departed with a very guilty mind. The next morning I returned to the shop, intending to pay for the apples. But before I could explain things, the man said, 'Had those two bream for supper.' They must have slipped out of my bag in my hasty departure, so we were quits, if you see what I mean.

At the hatches at Throop Weir Pool is a long, narrow bridge of about two feet wide that spans the river. One afternoon, having nothing better to do, I was watching salmon as they leapt out of the water.

There were two very stout women on the narrow bridge that I had hardly noticed, so far. Although, I was perhaps vaguely aware that they were leaning over the handrail of the said narrow bridge as I gazed across this wide weir pool. Suddenly, on the far side, a large salmon leapt out of its native element and landed in the rushes, three feet from the water's edge. What a free gift, I thought, as I dashed across the said narrow bridge. But, halfway across, I came to the two stout women, their rear portions bringing me to a sudden stop as they leaned upon the handrail. Slowly, the two stout women unbent themselves and stood erect, allowing me to pass, or just about. On I dashed, but I was one second too late, the salmon regained the pool and I had lost my prize, because of the two stout women.

Many years earlier, a party of salmon anglers asked me to go to Devon with them for a week's fishing, mainly on the River Taw. We stayed at the Fox and Hounds Hotel, which is right in the centre of the county and in a sparsely inhabited area. I had the same good service as did the other guests; also, each evening, I was given a pound to spend in the buffet nearby. Dinner was around 7 p.m., leaving little to do for most of the evening, so one would often linger in the buffet. This, of course, meant spending money. Should an angler be unlucky (I say "unlucky") to return with a salmon to the hotel, he had to treat everyone in the place to a drink.

There was one strange thing about this "treating" affair though, that I was never able to solve; it was like this: should you return proudly with a salmon, you would be asked to go straight to the buffet; here, you would find at least sixty thirsty natives awaiting you.

Some would have arrived on penny-farthing bikes, others astride horses. Now, how in the world did all these chaps know a salmon had been caught, because anyone fishing would be out of sight and far away in the wooded valley? Besides, usually no more than six or eight frequented the buffet. None of the thirsty ones had been "listening in", as it was long before telephones or wireless sets had become common in these isolated parts. So I got chatting to a gent from north of the border, who told me that he came every season, averaging four salmon a visit. He then went on to say that he was now almost bankrupt; a fish he had got that very day had cost him £4 15s in free drinks.

'You know,' he said, 'I once went straight to the little station here, intending to put my fish on the passenger train to Aberdeen. But when I got to the ticket office, there were already four fellows awaiting me and I was compelled to return to the hotel and order drinks – good old Scotch, too – for more than fifty of 'em.'

Seems there was no escape from "What will you have?"

In fact, aside from this said "treating spree", another thing I've never been able to solve is the mystery of the white donkey. But what a week that was in glorious Devon, in a county with such wonderful wooded landscape and a variety of coastal scenery. Perhaps one day I may go westwards again if one of my old employers should ask me to go once more. I shall not need asking twice.

31

The Hampshire Avon

In 1950, I left the Stour, because a new lessee took over the fishing rights. This newcomer very much wanted me to stay on, but he wanted me to break every rule of fishing. For instance, I was to tell the new salmon rods that we got 200 fish a season. I was also to catch any incoming salmon in the pools before the rods got on the water. He said, 'Fish from seven to ten o'clock each morning, before anyone turns up.' He also said, 'If you don't do as I say, out you go.'

This was enough; I went of my own accord to the Avon, near to Ringwood. Here, we (you recall that I now had a wife) were installed in Avon Castle as caretakers and to manage the fishing. During our first two years here, the castle was being turned into eight flats, so life was fairly pleasant. Part of the time I also looked after a length of nearby water for an old earl, who lived in a mansion.

We settled in, living in what at one time had been the staff's quarters at the rear of the castle. All our windows were heavily barred; this much puzzled me, as all the windows elsewhere had no iron bars. I was to find out the reason for this one afternoon, when two very old maids paid us a visit – they had worked here as parlour maids over fifty years ago.

I asked them why only the servants' rooms had iron bars to the windows and apparently, 'It was to keep we girls indoors. They was afraid that if we went out in the evenings, we would meet chaps and go courting and want to get married, so they would lose us.' Talk about the good old days. These iron bars were built into the stonework of the walls, so that one could not remove them; what a lot of daylight they kept out.

During the first two seasons here, I had some wonderful salmon fishing, catching fish for both the owner and his anglers, but I had other duties besides fishing, although on one or two odd occasions I was expressly asked to, 'Have a go.'

One morning, a lady came to fish and she landed one of 26 lb. Her husband, with two more anglers, had gone to fish the best beat on Lord Normanton's water at Ibsley; so, at noon, we put the salmon in the boot of her car and drove off to have lunch with the other party. We found them, although refrained from saying anything about our fish until after lunch; meanwhile, they teased us about wasting our time at the castle. They, however, had caught nothing. Then we showed t hem our fish; you should have seen their faces.

Near the White Gate Pool there was a cluster of rocks in the middle of the river. I recall a certain afternoon when I had been to Ringwood in my best clothes and shoes. On my way back, I had walked down river before tea to see if one of my rods was there. When I got there, I told him that I thought a fish might lie just ahead of the cluster of rocks, but that it was only reachable from a boat.

He told me to get my tea first, but I said, 'Now or never.'

So I took him off in the boat and went to the said spot. Within two minutes, he hooked a very big fish. I got the boat to the opposite bank and he climbed ashore to play the fish. But it went downstream and we had to follow; in fact, we went about 700 yards to a spot where we could go no farther, due to a swamp and some trees. Here, the fish slowed up. There was only one place I could reach it with my gaff, and that was by going into three feet of muddy water through the sedges, in my best shoes. Anyway, I went in and got the fish, all 35 lb of it.

After lunch one day I strolled off down to the fishing hut, when I thought I heard, faintly, a distant voice calling "Pond". Yes, there it was again. I grabbed my gaff in the hut and raced nearly a mile through three-foot high of standing grass. Reaching Oakford Wood, I found the same gent with a big salmon on his line, but he could not reach down to gaff it, as the river was very low, being June, and the bank was seven feet above the water.

I weighed up the situation, then I suggested, 'Suppose I lay down, my upper half being down the bank, you sit on me to prevent me going in and as soon as I get the gaff in the fish, you get one hand on the handle above my left hand, as I cannot take the full weight.'

We both nearly went in – but, somehow, we won and out came a 36½ lb salmon.

I can remember one cold, frosty morning when I crossed the river to fish the Summer House Pool – it was early in March. It got so cold that instead, I decided to walk nearly a mile to a pool that had only produced one fish in the past fifteen years. Reaching the spot, the river seemed to be flowing much too fast, so I just dropped my lure in to see if it was fishable. What a surprise, a salmon took the lure at once, after only three seconds of actual angling, 24 lb. It is such incidents as these that make fishing the finest pastime in the world.

When the flats at Avon Castle became occupied, I had the boilers to look after and a score of other duties. Gradually, more and more was put on me; the time came for me to leave. Except for one hour in the evenings, I was working seven days a week, 6.00 a.m. until 11.00 p.m. Thus I got an odd hour after tea for fishing.

In one flat was a lady with a daughter of about twenty-one; this girl was keen to learn how to cast. Now I've taught hundreds all the various methods of casting, so I kept a very old rod and reel for the purpose – these learners are very unkind to good tackle, and to keepers, too, the flying hooks being known to catch you in the ear'ole or pants.

One evening, I found time to take this lass to the river. She spent half an hour flogging the water; really, to tell the truth, she did not do too badly. In fact, she was so mad keen that the next evening, we again went down to the river. Handing her my old gear, she made a bad cast (?), the lure only went out two yards and a fish took it straight away. Throwing the rod at me, she tripped over her heresy on the bank, regained her feet and rushed into the castle shouting, 'I've caught a fish.' I continued to play it, but, somehow, I sensed that it was but lightly hooked. By the time she got back, I was about to gaff it, offered her the rod and said I would soon land it for her, but no, she wanted to gaff it. I gave in and let her do so. She got it out perfectly and the lure fell out of its mouth as it lay on the grass, 28 lb. I have said before, salmon fishing is fifty per cent luck and fifty per cent skill. Well, perhaps it was a bit of both in this instance.

There is more than one way of getting a salmon. Up north, a gang of poachers will go to a pool, taking a dead rabbit, its ears having been cut off, and they then tie one end of a long, thin rope to its neck. The rabbit is then dropped into the lower end of the pool and the other end of the rope is taken to the top of the pool. A couple of members of the gang would take up positions on one side of the pool and another two on the other side, each with a gaff. Another man would then pull the rabbit through the entire length of the pool. The salmon, thinking it to be an otter, would dash madly into the shallow areas and the four men with gaffs would pull out several of them.

Now having let the cat (or rabbit) out of the bag, don't you dare try any tricks; it's you that will be caught. Now here's a tip, for what it is worth: two tins of sardines – having removed top dressing of dead cats and old sardine tins – oh, sorry, I've mixed this up with another "plot". To continue, open one tin and scatter a few sardines on the water, now use sardines from the second tin for baiting up. You will be surprised if you catch anything at all, so shall I, perhaps better to get the lawn cut.

32

Salmon Anglers I've Known

One old toff, bringing his butler, would arrive at our fishing hut about noon, both fully laden with tackle. I would stay in the hut with them talking for about an hour and then the old toff would suggest, 'What about lunch?' So I would go home and come back again at about two o'clock. There would be another hour of talking, all about salmon, of course, and then at around three o'clock, some six or seven casts were made. Then we would return to the hut for more nattering: feel a bit tired, can't go on, must rest; then we'll pack up. Some people call this "fishing". Yes, I've met all sorts.

There was one chap with whom I often went after the mighty salmon. He was forever telling me about the one which had got away. After about the eighteenth time of hearing it all over again, he looked at me for some expression of sympathy when he'd finished, but he got none; you see, I was actually present when he had lost the fish, seems he had forgotten that.

This same chap had been fishing the Chestnut Pool one evening, a tree being on the opposite bank and a large round bush on our side. A fish rose two yards upstream of the bush, so he dashed round the bush to cast, but it then rose once more, only below the bush this time, so back he rushed. I went above the bush and heaved in a big stone, causing him to rush back again, thinking the splash must be the salmon. I heaved another stone in below the bush and back he rushed round to the other side again. This went on a dozen times or more, until, finally, he began to wonder why there was a heap of clean-looking stones in the river either side of the bush and no sign of a salmon.

Another odd incident worth telling was the time when one of my salmon anglers had a week's holiday. His wife would be away at the time, so what better than a week at the river? Apart from feeding himself and the two cats, there was little else to do at home, just a few household duties between visits to the river; we shall see.

I met him on his first day out and had a chat, wherein I was obliged to tell him that very few fish had come in from the sea. But as the days passed, I would find him somewhere casting away. In fact, he was fishing all hours, he so badly wanted to land a salmon, but all he could boast of were two small pike.

By the time Saturday came round, his last day, there was no bed made, no crocks washed-up and no carpets swept, but to the river he went – all day he toiled. He looked at his watch, 6 p.m., wife due back at 8.45 p.m. He would stay just another half-hour; then it happened, a fish took hold and after a long fight, a 27 lb salmon was landed. All he had time for was to dash home, get all the washing-up done, the bed neatly made, the food back into the pantry, etc., before she returned. All as simple as that.

But when he reached home, he found the front door open and a light in the dining room; yes, his wife had come back on an earlier train and her greeting was anything but cordial. After ten minutes non-stop moaning, she finished by saying, 'And to think that I went to the expense of buying two nice cutlets of fresh salmon, only to find the place in a terrible state when I get back; what a fool I am to have gone.'

The angler, at a loss for words, picked up the salmon cutlets and gave them to the two cats, and then poured a stiff brandy for his wife, seems she needed it badly. Then he went back to his car to get the fish, dumping it upon the dining room table on his return – the kitchen sink was far too congested. Soon, all peace reigned and all was forgiven; a happy ending to what might have otherwise been a different story.

The moral of the story is obvious; when the wife is away, keep the kitchen sink and draining board clear of dirty crocks, if only because a dining-room table is not exactly a suitable place to deposit a wet, muddy and bloodstained salmon.

One night, when Muggy called in for a chat, we were joined later by old Fryer, the Boscombe longshoreman, who had a long white beard and wore a faded cap and jersey.

'What about having a day off the Needles?' he asked.

So the next morning, the three of us met at Mudeford and set sail in Fryer's boat. Now, I shall have little to say of the day – it's what happened at night that may be of interest. Though I will add that we had something like 120 lb of fish: bream, whiting and dabs.

It was late when we came ashore and with having so much fish to carry, we left our tackle in the boathouse. Fryer was soon away on his ancient motorbike; Muggy and I only had cycles and an eight-mile ride before us. We had ridden nearly two miles, when Muggy suggested taking a short cut through a military camp. We did just that and as we were about to pass the guardroom there was a terrific report, Muggy's back tyre had burst at that precise moment. The sentry dropped his rifle, out rushed the entire guard and we were marched, or rather dragged, bikes and all, into the Orderly Room, which, of course, began to look rather disorderly.

The sergeant had quite a lot to say and this is only the half of it: 'We've had reports of three shops bin broken into, one was a fish shop, none o' our blokes, must ring the police.' Then we heard him say to the police: 'We got 'em red-handed; they got the fish wiv 'em.'

A couple of policemen arrived promptly – we, of course, must be guilty, as we had no fishing tackle, so off we all went to the police station, where we were asked many questions for over an hour. Then, at last, they agreed to take us to the boathouse and to call at Fryer's home in Haviland Road to confirm matters. We showed them our tackle and the fish scales on the bottom boards and at last it came about that a fishermen's tale was actually believed and we were conveyed, cycles and all, to our doorsteps. I think we all saw the funny side of it.

A couple of days later, Muggy and I met old Fryer in Boscombe Arcade. Astonished passers-by saw three old salts laughing their heads off. We were talking about the night before the night before. Then we all went to the pictures – to see *Three Men in a Boat*.

My opinion of Specimen Hunters is that first and foremost, these fellows get very few of the real big 'uns and they waste much of their time getting next to nothing – they would be better occupied in catching fish by the old-fashioned and proved methods. More than half of the specimens were taken before 1946, and there were only half the number of anglers then than there is now. You just need to look at any specimen list dating from 1898 for the facts.

In a lifetime, by sea and river, I've had to deal with thousands of anglers and I know full well that it is the beginner and usually the young lad, who gets the outsized fish; the angling press proves this to be so, if you consistently follow the reports. It seems that those fellows who boast of being Specimen Hunters must have a one-track mind; they are missing the real joys of our sport, just to enable them to have a chance of getting their name in print. Some recent specimen lists quote weights so low that they almost get a foot on the bottom of the ladder; some of these fellows do not even get that far, it's the happy-go-lucky ones or the boys who get right to the top. The only real specimen taken by an expert was by Dick Walker, which was a carp of 44 lb, and that was a long time ago. I, like so many other chaps, have taken many large fish of most species, all caught by accident and not by design. I can look back to two black bream, 4 lb 8 oz, and 4 lb 5 oz, also two plaice each over 7 lb and two dace both 1 lb 3 oz but I've never made a song about it.

These specimen hunters write hundreds of articles telling us what bait, what size of hook and what length of rod you must use. You read the same old thing over and over again. Yet, I've used the same rod and same reel for over twenty years for every type of fishing, both sea and river. One writer takes over a hundred things to the river; I take ten and get my fish. No wonder boys are put off our sport, being told they must have loads of expensive tackle – they have not got the money for it.

33

"Fetch my Rod!"

A little way back I mentioned that I also looked after a length of water downstream, which belonged to an old earl. With having so much work to do at Avon Castle, I had to give this up. One day, however, the earl approached my employers to ask if I could come and fish his water on a certain Thursday, as a large party was to be held in the mansion and fresh salmon was a must on the menu. With little hope of getting a fish to order, I went, only to find the earl in rather a bad mood. 'Must have a fish today, d'you hear,' he shouted. So off I hastened to the river.

I fished for four solid hours, and not a single fish showed; in fact, they had been few and far between for the past two weeks. At 2 p.m., I sat down for a sandwich, but by 2.15 p.m., the old earl came along in a terrible rage, accusing me of wasting my time, adding, 'Fetch my rod.'

This, I did, but worse was to follow. On his third cast, he hooked a fish, seemed to be a day when I could do nothing right. I felt exactly like that little word in "embarrassment", but wait; soon, things were going to change. The earl talked all the while, telling the fish what it should do, and what a river keeper ought to do, and what a feast there would be that night for the 200 guests. But that salmon was a big and lively one and when seventy yards of line had been reeled out, the backing broke. Was I sorry or glad? I don't know. For some moments, the earl was speechless; I could find nothing to say, either. Then at last he threw his rod down and exploded.

'Bring my tackle to the house and a salmon with it, or ...' and, adding nothing more, he strode away.

There seemed to be little hope of a fish, but within fifteen minutes, I hooked a small one. With great care, I played it. But how very odd – it would only swim five yards up river and five yards down, which it proceeded to do scores of times. When I fished it out, I found the reason for these antics – several yards of line were wrapped around the salmon's head, the same kind of line that the earl had been using.

After killing the fish, I rejoined this line to the earl's reel, which was not far away. Then, winding up some slack, I found a fish to be on the other end of it. Going into battle again, I began to play this fish and after about twenty minutes, had it on the bank, 29 lb on my spring balance. Must hasten to the mansion, surely I would be made more welcome than any of the noble guests.

So with two rods, two gaffs, two bags and two salmon, out of breath, I staggered up the massive steps to the front entrance, bespattered in mud and blood, and rang the great bell with such energy that the chain came away in my hands. The entire household, led by the earl, came rushing through the lobby. I was, indeed, made welcome – two quarts of ale were set before me, with the old earl seated beside me, after phoning my employers to tell them that I must have another day to fish for myself and keep the fish – if any. Leaving the mansion after a third quart "for the road", (it was only a narrow drive) I went straight home; well, nearly straight home.

The next day, I began angling like mad at 7.00 a.m. By eleven o'clock, I was less hopeful and stopped for a while. Then at noon, I started again, hooked a small fish and landed it within a few minutes. Soon after this, another fish showed, must be a run on, I thought. But no more luck. I went home to tea. Later, I got the urge to go to the river. Within a few minutes, I took one of 17 lb. I fished on until dark, when a fish showed, so I put a luminous type of spinner on and got a small pull, but it was only a pike of about 3 lb. A handful of swans approached, but seeing my shining lure coming through the air, they thought was a comet and departed. I continued to cast, had a tug, but missed it. Then I had a heavy pull and began a struggle that lasted a full half-hour. By the time I got the fish alongside, I could not see it in the darkness, so had to feel with the gaff; by sheer luck, I had lifted out a salmon of 24 lb. A total of three fish in one day (and part night) – never done it before.

The next day, I presented the smallest salmon (14 lb) to the old earl, I think I owed it to him, and implored him to get a new and reliable line of at least 150 yards; the word "backing" often means a losing game; I am not talking about horses, mind. The 17 lb fish was cut up into suitable portions to be shared with numerous relatives (what a lot of them there seemed to be), and the twenty-four-pounder was sold to defray expenses – my line was a bit frayed, too, so it was time to buy a new one.

What is it like, playing a big salmon?

All the while you are thinking – did I tie that knot securely; wonder if the backing is still strong enough? You tremble as your fish nearly gets foul of a sunken branch. By now, you are not only perspiring, you are nearly expiring. Your mind is in turmoil, oh, the agony of it all, how will it all end? You eventually fumble for the gaff, but your two hands are insufficient and you really need six hands. The gaff slips from your fingers and while picking it up, you get a boot full of water.

Even the fish is feeling as bad as you do – it comes slowly in, belly-up. You struggle up the muddy bank with it and you, too, lay belly-up and recover. Fit again? Yes, the happiest moment of your life.

Now for some sobering thoughts: when a keeper is with his gent, he has several things to keep in mind while a fish is being played. He has to reckon with any low branches overhead and also see that other vegetation does not foul the line. The angler's feet must also be watched, to avoid stumbling on uneven ground, or tripping over obstacles. The keeper must urge his angler to get below the fish, as this gives the hooks a more secure hold; it also means the fish has to combat the current. When played downstream, it will not tire so quickly, simply because it need not waste energy in swimming against the stream. Both men should keep away from the water's edge until it is time to use the gaff or tailer. Small hooks will hold bigger fish more securely, because with big hooks, the fish grip the shank and roll it between their hard lips, thus loosening the hold.

Looking across the river one very hot day, I saw a gent fishing. Owing to the heat, he had undone his belt, and soon he had hooked a salmon. Whilst playing it, his pants started to descend, so to prevent them from falling right down, he was obliged to play his fish in one position, with his knees pressed together. Although thus handicapped, he still got his fish.

I recall a morning when I took a wealthy gent across our river to fish the Summer House Pool; so far, after two seasons, he had failed to land a salmon. Also with us was the manager of his factory, who had assisted him to the bank with all the gear. The gent got his first fish, 20 lb; to celebrate, be opened a large bottle of whisky and emptied it. I had the job of bringing the three of us back across the river, and the fish and the gear, in a very tiny boat. How we got over, I can't tell; however, I know that when I stepped ashore to hold the boat steady, I sat down heavily in some very soft mud.

The imprint of my rear anatomy remained visible throughout the remainder of that long, dry summer.

34

Funny Things Occur

I've had many a laugh by river and sea at the strange things that happen to anglers and me.

Having been talking of castles and mansions, it has reminded me of an incident in my early days back at Andover. In a village nearby was a stately mansion. We youngsters used to peer through the massive iron gates at the great house within. Sometimes, we would dare to creep in to have a look at the carp in the lake, and then utter loud, complimentary remarks such as: 'Coo, luvelly', 'Ain't it posh,' 'Look at that big 'un.' Whereupon the butler would rush out and yell, 'Clear off, we don't want your sort, begone.' These days, I'm one of the "your sort" and provided I have half a crown, I am actually invited through those massive gates to a day's carp fishing.

On one recent visit, the fishing suddenly stopped, four chaps went off with a van and were caught by the duke in the act of taking away 14 huge carp, which had been placed in two tanks in the van. Needless to say, all the fish had to be put back.

One day, I was stood in a pool testing a fly rod of excellent quality. Anyway, my fly got caught up in a branch overhead (yes, I am a duffer), and I could not see where it was, so I asked a yokel on the bridge if he could see it.

'Aye, ther' it be, wer' yer stock's pointin',' he said. Shades of Hardy Bros comes to mind.

Another time, I was hurrying to the river with a crowd of anglers for a competition. I got talking to one chap when we became parted in the rush, just as he was saying, '… then I had nearly got the fish in the net –!' It was not until two years later, that I saw him again, and he started a conversation like this: '… when the blighter jumped out and got away.' Somehow, I got away, too. If ever a chap had the fishing bug, this one had it – it's contagious, you know; but please don't drop this book – it's not fatal.

In the following story, the first part is ordinary and fishy, the latter part unique and true. One of my regular anglers came for a day's fishing and told me that he had landed a 9 lb bass at Mudeford, and lost one of about 15 lb, or so he said. I doubted the latter part of his story, having heard of the one that got away so often, however, I agreed to go for a day's bass fishing on the next Friday with both him and another fellow.

Now you may know, or not know, that bass only seek for food near the shore when the sea is rough. But when we got there, it could not have been a more hopeless day, the sea was flat and gin clear and the heat intense. We hung our three lunch bags on a tree in the shade, just beyond the sand dunes. Some four hours passed, but not a fish to show for it. At last, we decided to seek the shade of the tree where we had left our lunch bags, to eat and drink the contents. But upon reaching the tree, we had a rude shock. There, on the ground, lay three empty bags – the food had all been consumed and the three beer bottles were empty, too.

Climbing a sandhill, we saw a tramp rapidly disappearing inland. All three of us gave chase, but it was useless. Have you ever tried a cross-country race in rubber thigh boots? So, on returning home, we had a sad tale to relate about the one that got away.

You may recall the time when I fished for the earl. Well, just about a year before I came to the Avon, he gave a big party, because his daughter was "Coming Out" – what she had been in for I don't know. Anyhow, it was another occasion when no less than four salmon were wanted, as about 260 guests were going there expecting a feast.

So far, salmon were so scarce that local shops could not get any, so the earl sent his closest friends to the river to catch some. They fished long and hard, but you know how hopeless it can be sometimes, and not a fish could they catch. The bottom pool was not fished; the rather temperamental bull in the field there had a dislike of people waving long sticks – again shades of Hardy Bros.

Now, something strange happened at that pool on the night before the party. A gang of poachers (taking a truss of hay to pacify the bull) netted this famous, yet neglected pool. They took out eleven salmon, which they then put on the early-morning train to Billingsgate. Meanwhile, the old earl was raving mad, still with no fish for his guests; he even went down to the pool where the bull was standing, but not a fish was to be had. All the while, the huge animal stood watching and remained passive; perhaps it felt compassion for the old man. What a tale it could tell, could it have spoken.

Reaching home, there was only one thing the earl could do, phone the London wholesalers to send four fish by passenger train. Four of those eleven fish made the return journey yes, you might say, "they had been taken for a ride". The old earl had paid dearly for what had been his fish in his own water.

Looking back over the years, I realise that our rivers do not hold as many fish, of such average weight, as they did in the early days of this century. Pollution has become the main reason; the time when we could catch around 100 lb of mixed fish in a few hours has gone. Today, despite so much refined tackle and books and articles telling us just how to catch 'em, we either have blank days or perhaps a mere twenty or forty fish. Only at sea do you stand a chance of getting a worthwhile catch.

There are now nearly three million anglers in the British Isles. If this number increases much more, we shall look like being limited to catching one fish per annum, perhaps. It might even come to this: when you catch your one (and only) fish, you attach a small, metal disc to the anal fin with a number on it, and don't forget to give the disc a kink; this will make the fish go round in circles. You will already have paid sixpence to the Anglers' Co-operative Association (you mangy cad), or some other society, to obtain the numbered disc. You then sign on at the Exchange until the next season arrives and when you sign off, you go back to the spot where you returned that fish.

Now should you catch that same fish, on producing the disc, you will receive £75,000. It saves the bother of having to find eight noughts or crosses. The odds, oddly enough, are about the same, so there's no need to order a glass case just yet. Anyway, I wish you luck – you'll need it. I would like to see representatives of all nations sit round the table in agreement – if such a big table exists.

How peaceful the animals and birds can be. Early one morning, I came to a board that spanned a stream – on it sat a badger and a cat, and just below, a duck was on the water. Outside my window was a wheelbarrow and looking out very early one morning, I saw three birds perched upon it: a woodpecker, a dipper and a kingfisher. If you live in out-of-the-way places like I have done, you discover many of nature's little secrets.

For instance, moles know weeks beforehand that a flood will come and spread over the water-meadows, and here and there you may notice some very huge mole hills, some two or three feet high – these are safety refuges. Herons do not only eat fish, they are partial to water rats and field mice. The only time they are a nuisance is when you have a baby trout in a stew pond, but they can be kept away by placing an alarm clock on a biscuit tin. If you set the alarm to go off at about sunrise, the resulting din is terrific in the stillness of the dawn. That heron will never come back again.

> A lively young fisher named Fischer,
> Fished for fish from the edge of a fissure,
> When a fish with a grin
> Pulled that fisherman in,
> Now they are fishing that fissure for Fischer.

35

Life in an Old Mill

Things got so bad at Avon Castle that my wife and I could not cope with so many jobs. Both of us were fully engaged for seven days a week, at all hours of each day. So we moved to a mill at Dinton in South Wiltshire on the River Nadder, where I took charge of three miles of trout fishing, also a large lake containing carp and perch. Up to 1946, the Nadder gave me my two best dace, both weighing in at 1 lb each, and then in 1948, I had two more, 1 lb 3 oz and 1 lb 2½ oz. Yes I had my moments.

Talk about being isolated. It was nearly as bad as those years when I was on the lonely heath. We were a long way from any road, we had to fetch our meat, milk and newspapers, and we also had to burn oil lamps, with having no electricity or gas. When a bad flood came, we were marooned in the mill for several days; no postman or tradesmen could reach us, nor would the ancient machinery bake us a loaf, and there was no flour, either. These floods would rise suddenly. One afternoon, my wife had to attend a Women's Institute meeting, as she was the president, but when she returned, she was unable to reach the mill due to a sudden rise in water level, so she had to stay the night in a village. This also happened when she had to attend a meeting in Salisbury. There were also occasions when our well was contaminated by muddy water from the nearby river.

But despite all these drawbacks, we were to spend seven years here and never to regret it. We had come to the Nadder Valley, a most peaceful and natural area, away from the bustle and wickedness of the world beyond; there was every kind of bird and wild flower and no one to sell us bootlaces.

My employer was a real gentleman and had an estate not very far away. Near his big house was a lake and a few of the local fellows were allowed to fish it. Never have I known such an easy place to catch big carp; I took nine in one morning once, all double-figure weights, using the soft part of the top of a cottage loaf as bait. On hot days, huge shoals would come and lie on the shallows. These lazy fish would move away when I landed with the boat, but they would soon be back again.

Permits to fish had to be stopped for a while as regards night fishing, due to a party of fellows, who came with a lorry with which to take away their big catch of carp. We made them put the fish back in the lake, but had we let them take fish away, no doubt other parties would have come along to do exactly the same thing and thus deplete his stock of carp. Four days after this affair, I found a dead carp of between 20 and 25 lb possibly it had not recovered from being placed in the lorry, so I buried it nearby.

There must have been about a million tiny perch in the lake, none more than 4 oz, stunted due to a lack of suitable food. Many thousands were netted out by the River Board and were taken to rivers where they had a chance to grow bigger. The extent of the lake was about 400 yards in length and 150 yards in width. Any overflow passed on to our trout stream by way of a hatch at the north end. Here, the depth was 10½ feet, graduating at the opposite end to a mere 10 inches. In the centre was a small island seventy-five by forty-five feet, which was heavily overgrown with brambles and a few trees. Later, I cut all this growth back and burned it. This little isle was inhabited by a colony of moles; how they ever arrived there was a mystery. We obtained 100 trout and put them in the lake there, but never saw a trout afterwards; it's anybody's guess as to what happened to them, and there were no pike present to eat these trout.

Although there were plenty of trout in our river, it was also packed with grayling, roach, dace and pike; this was due to the ample supply of natural food present. I took out hundreds of these fish with my rod, but it made little difference, so I sought the help of the River Board again. They came on several occasions and netted out many thousands of coarse fish; these were also transferred to rivers where there was a shortage of stock.

One morning, I came upon two otters dining on a pike which they had captured. They soon made off and I dropped the pike back in the river onto a ledge. The bank here was four feet high, so how these otters had got it up the steep slope was a mystery. I decided to come back the next day to see if they had returned for another meal and sure enough, I found them both there, with the pike once more on top of the bank; the fish must have originally weighed about 22 lb.

There are four rivers join the Avon at Salisbury; they are the Nadder, Ebble, Bourne and Wyle. On each of these streams – or call them rivers if you prefer – an immense amount of weed cutting is done. This weed drifts all the way down the Avon to the sea, ruining the fishing prospects all the way. More recently, this weed has been taken out by a mechanical elevator at certain places and thus huge piles accumulate. As this weed rots, a liquid flows from it back into the river and pollutes the water; if the weed could be spread over adjoining fields, it might do some good, as it has manurial properties.

Despite this bulk extraction of weed, there are still thousands of short lengths adrift all the time. Bits of these get caught up on both sides of the river, and a rise of water or change of wind will tend to release these pieces; also, those that have collected at hatches are set free when water levels are raised or lowered. The amount of weed cut in the Avon is nearly 1,000 tons per mile. Most of this has been extracted now, but, years back, I've known such large amounts to become entangled on the chains of yachts moored in the Christchurch estuary that craft were carried away.

Banks of this weed used to pile up all round the bay and rot, attracting millions of flies. But things are improving now, as the weed is only being "topped" – it is just the longer lengths that are cut. Weed, of course, puts oxygen into the water and provides cover and food for the fish, to destroy it is contrary to nature. I've been on about this matter for years, but my small voice has had but little effect.

My employer and one or two of his friends used to go to the lower Avon, salmon fishing. I used to go, too, in the Rolls-Royce. How I enjoyed those days. True, we never got many fish, as the river had two poor seasons, but we got the odd salmon. I was also able to indicate certain likely spots and a catch would sometimes result.

Catching salmon really does spoil desire to go after other fish and I soon tired of carp fishing at the lake, they are ugly brutes to look at and put up little fight. It is the same with bream, which are covered in slime; tench is another odd-looking fish, fond of muddy haunts.

Longshoreman

Once you've had a trout of 5 lb plus a 4 lb plaice, or a bass of 10 lb, or even a 9 lb salmon, you know what's worth catching.

I never use a keepnet, what is the sense of jamming scores of fish into such a confined space? Seldom do I carry a landing net; I prefer to lift out my quarry – tiddler-snatching is not sport, far from it. In fact, it should be banned from competitions, because these tiny fish suffer injuries through being hastily unhooked and thrown into a keepnet.

One evening, I saw an angler turn his net inside out to return his catch; forty odd roach plunged back into the river. The next morning, I could see about fifteen tails sticking up out of the mud. With the water being only thirty inches deep, these fish had shot straight into the soft mud and had suffocated.

I often liked to angle under a shady oak, as it was possible to see all the fish and no float was necessary. From there, I could see my bait and draw it away from a tiddler; but if it was a big roach I would also draw it away, slowly, as this made roach go for it.

36

Visit to Weymouth

It is perhaps fortunate that most people who can read your mind happen to be good-natured people, otherwise they would certainly biff you one when reading your evil mind.

I have already related some of the escapades I have had with Muggy, but, one morning, a letter came from him, suggesting that we had a day on Chesil Beach, near Weymouth. He would dig up some worms and come by bus to Salisbury, where we would take another bus to the Naples of England, as it is known. There was no time to reply, as his letter said "tomorrow". So, the next morning, I arrived in Salisbury; Muggy was already there.

'You're early, I think,' I remarked.

'Hitch-hiked,' was his reply.

Now I never had the nerve to do this sort of thing and said, in a very abrupt tone, 'Come on, we buy two return tickets.'

Muggy opened his mouth, but words did not seem to come out of it at first, then he blurted out, 'I've forgot to bring any money.'

I am sure he could read my own evil thoughts right then, but there was no going back now, he had the bait, we had packed our tackle and food, so I paid for the two return fares. Reaching Weymouth, I again forked out, buying four bottles of beer and some extra bait, upon which Muggy gazed with great approval, saying, 'We shall need all that and more.'

At the time, it failed to dawn on me as to what he really meant, but I was to find out some hours later.

Reaching the famous Chesil Beach, we cast out and looked forward to a pleasant day's fishing. But the fish refused to oblige, not that it worried Muggy, he had laid deep plans of which I knew nowt – being slow on the old uptake.

Chesil Beach; what a wonderful place this is, stretching fifteen miles to the west and acting as a protective barrier to much of the Dorset coast when heavy seas surge shorewards. At Bridport, which is at the extreme westerly end of this long beach, there is only very small shingle, but as you come back in an easterly direction, mile by mile, you will notice that the shingle gradually becomes small pebbles and that the pebbles gradually begin to increase in size. By the time you near Weymouth, they become almost boulders. There is a reason for this; the prevailing south-westerly winds drive heavy seas shorewards, this causes the larger stones to be carried eastwards; exactly the same thing occurs and is noticeable along other south-coast bays. But the day we went to Chesil Beach, it could only show pebbles by the million and not a single fish.

We fished all day, and at last, I said, 'Better be going, got to get that last bus.'

Never before had I known Muggy take so long to pack up. It was a long, tiring walk to the bus station and when we arrived, we were just in time to see the last bus going out.

'Muggy, let me see your watch.'

It was forty minutes slow, and we were forty miles from Salisbury. He would still have farther to travel than I would, even when allowing for my extra nine miles out to Dinton Mill. The train service was no good, and nor did I have enough money for the two fares if there had been a train, only having about fifteen bob on my person at that time.

'What's to do?' Muggy muttered in a jubilant undertone, and then added, 'Go fishing?'

I could have chucked him to the crabs had we been upon that shore, but there were other things to do. First, I must phone a friend in Dinton and ask him to inform my wife that we would be back next day. I then offered Muggy the last of the coppers to phone his home.

He simply remarked, 'But I'm not expected back until tomorrow, thanks for offering to pay though.'

Slow on the uptake? Yes, I must have been; if only I had brought my watch, but sea air did not agree with it, and nor did it agree with me at that very moment. We would have to go back to the beach for the night, as we could not afford the price of hotels.

The night was becoming colder, so we went to an inn, where we were able to warm up and get something to eat and drink. I also paid for extra rations to see us through the night. When the natives in the inn heard that we would be going fishing, they one and all told us how wonderful the sport would be. Upon hearing this, Muggy fished out a torch from the bottom of his bag. The bulb proved to be useless, so an old netsman went out and fetched an oil lamp, which we agreed to return in the morning, he having filled it up with oil and we having filled him up with beer.

So back to the beach we went, with that hope which you may already know springs forever in the angler's heart. The tide had begun to rise and we commenced fishing in earnest, but, with the exception of small pout and ling, the sport was poor. By midnight, we were fed up and shivering from the cold, so we searched the upper beach for driftwood and soon had a fire going. We dined on potato crisps, biscuits and beer, and soon felt much happier and, with lots of wood at hand, we kept a big fire going. Resuming his fishing, Muggy played his last card.

Turning his bag upside down, he produced a box containing three dozen razorfish, saying: 'Got 'em at Sandbanks, fish can see a whitebait on pebbles yards away, small work hooks do slide down 'tween stones out o' sight.'

Well, I cannot say whether it was the light reflecting from our fire or the change of bait, but we started catching fish almost at once – plaice, bass, whiting and codling, nothing under one and a half pound, except for the whiting and these were a fair size, too. By 5 a.m., we had about 45 lb of fish, at which point Muggy put the last bit of razorfish on his rod, cast out and came and sat by the fire. All at once, my rod bell rang. Hastily rushing into action, I was soon playing a big fish, a bass, I felt sure. When at last I got it ashore, we found that the fish had taken a hook on Muggy's trace. It appeared that when he had cast out, he had failed to put on his check; the bass had become hooked and had fouled my line. I wonder if Muggy could read my thoughts by the faint light of the approaching dawn. Did he really deserve a bass of nearly ten and a half pounds? Perhaps he did, after all.

A couple of hours later, we went back and returned the lamp to the old netsman, plus about 14 lb of fish. A barrow boy paid us sixteen shillings for most of the remaining catch – we could not carry them all on the bus anyway. Muggy kept his big bass, and I a codling of 7 lb, and a prime dab of 1 lb 9 oz.

This trip was made when at Dinton Mill. Muggy is now away in Geelong, South Australia, where he rides round on horseback, inspecting agricultural machinery. He was getting £40 a week (in 1957), I was getting less than a quarter of that sum, being slow on the uptake as you will already have realised, but I am privy to the green meadows and fast gliding streams.

My thoughts often go back to salt water, to the early days when a bag of eighty or ninety tiny smelts was common; how delicious they were. Then I recall trips under sail for thresher sharks, mainly in Studland Bay or off Ballard Head. My party had some specimens, 266 and 262 lb were the best; Mr Butler took most of the threshers, Mitchell-Hedges lost most of his big ones. But as I said before, dogfish, tope and suchlike has no lasting appeal to me, and nor do sharks. Frankly, I was bored stiff when after these monsters, I prefer a 4 lb plaice.

In 1960, the lease of the fishing at the mill expired – so did I, almost – then, by a stroke of good fortune, I heard of a post on the renowned Hampshire Test.

37

The Anchor is Let Go

So it came about that in 1961, we moved to Wherwell, four miles south of Andover. I took the post as head river keeper for the Countess of Brecknock, Priory Estate, Wherwell, on the famous River Test. Yes, I had come back to within 4 miles of the town in which I was born, where, at the age of four, I got the urge to go a-fishing again. Nearly sixty years has gone by since I had left "Garden by the River".

Often, I catch the bus to Andover and every time, I have to go and look across the Anton River at the old garden from which I caught many a fine trout. In the front of our large old house are now three shops; these were built on what had been our lawn. The mighty two chestnut trees are no more and the red may tree has also gone. But the river still flows silently on to join the Test not far from Wherwell. Somehow, Andover does not appeal to me now, perhaps it is because of the constant stream of motor traffic going in both directions through Bridge Street, the sight of shops on our old lawn and the row of cars parked at the river's side. Even the large back garden on the opposite bank is now overgrown with weeds and ragged bushes, and the old summer house lies collapsed under a huge mass of ivy; the boathouse is also no more.

No, I don't like it any more, but the little river still appeals, and the town mill just upstream, but the few trout are very small – there just isn't the stock of fish as there were in days of old, those days when almost every trout was a two-pounder. There also aren't many big trout at Wherwell. Much of the Test has but a few large fish – only on one or two sections can you find trout of three to five pound and these have been hand fed and probably obtained from fish farms. The once famous Test is no longer famous. The use of artificial manures on the land has destroyed much fish life, also the food they depend on. Poaching still goes on above my water and near Romsey.

With my under-keepers, we have plenty to do though, eight miles of banks have to be cut three times a year, fallen trees have to be removed, silt needs to be extracted, river weed to be maintained, overhanging branches to be cut, fences, stiles, bridges and hatches to be maintained, pike and grayling to be removed and snags to be located and taken out. But river keepers do not work to fixed hours; there is still that sort of freedom which I have enjoyed for over sixty years. We do not get bored with a job, if we want a change, we turn to some other kind of work, and there is always plenty of interest when working with nature.

A few salmon came up as far as Wherwell, but they would be out of condition, not worth catching, although I was lucky to be offered three days' fishing near Romsey, where I got a fresh-run fish each day – 15, 12 and 9½ lb, which were small in comparison to those I got on other rivers. In my four years here, I took eighty-seven pike, spinning, best two 16 and 15 lb, also some grayling over 2 lb. On a few occasions, I went to Southampton Waters and Ryde sea fishing, but did not get many fish, as it was always difficult to get bait and the right tides.

The Duke of Edinburgh sometimes shot over our estate. One day, the guns were all lined up ready to move off. You never saw such an assortment of coloured stockings as the gents were wearing; one had brilliant red ones. It is reputed that the Duke was heard to say, 'Glad to see all nations are represented.' On one particular shoot, we had the queen walking around our village most of the day and nobody recognised her – she must have been glad of that though.

Due to the shortage of fish in inshore waters, increasing numbers of gulls are coming many miles inland to feed on fish in our rivers. We kept trying to drive them off, but when your particular stretch of water is four miles long, you can't be everywhere all the time. Even cormorants are coming thirty miles up some of our rivers; each bird can eat its own weight each day. Perhaps it is no wonder that the Test, also the Itchen, contain less fish, as pollution and agricultural manuring of the meadows and fields has reduced life, not only in these two rivers, but also in most other rivers. When I was on both the Avon and the Stour, I could get immediate advice and assistance if there was any fish mortality; here, on this river, nobody seems concerned if fish are found dead.

I've been told that my life has been unique, if only because of my total of thirty-two years on the coast and another thirty-two years at the riverside, also for living most of my life rent-free. Only at Goathorn Hamlet did I pay rent for a few years, and that was only one shilling and sixpence per week, with no rates, and when on *Thalassa*, the harbour dues were no more than £4 per year.

I have caught many specimens over my time and you can't help it if you land some real big ones, and another thing was that they were all caught by accident; had I tried to get only the larger fish, I would have done no better, probably much worse. Some carp anglers spend all night in mist and cold trying to lure one big carp. Some succeed, some don't, yet I went to that Wiltshire lake and could get a dozen or more in a morning, as did others who had a permit.

We read articles by fellows who could land a chub of 4 lb; nothing remarkable about doing this, nor in catching a net full of bream, they come in like logs and cover your hands with slime. I have some sympathy for barbel fanatics, a ten-pounder is a good one, but rarely do they get one this size, and only then perhaps after many wasted days. For the specimen lists, I would suggest the following minimum weights – carp 28 lb, bream 8 lb, chub 6 lb and barbel 12 lb.

I have never specialised (except for salmon, which is an entirely different procedure) and nor have I carried around a vast amount of tackle. All my fishing gear is crude and ancient, my one and only rod since 1942 has been an eight feet four inch tubular steel one, the reel a centre-pin three and a half inches in diameter, yet many thousands of fish have been landed with this combination. From about 1922 until 1942, I used a cheap rod of seven feet and an old Nottingham reel daily; these remained in a boat for nearly all those years, sometimes immersed in rainwater for hours at a time and other times when it was frozen in a cake of ice.

Yes, I've had it the hard way, but never regretted a day; in fact, I've had more fun out of my fishing than most people. Perhaps my success

157

was because I went after the fish, I did not bother about the popular marks, river or sea; for example, I never fished a salmon pool, always the neck or tail ends of pools and the special small ones lie elsewhere in the river.

My methods were often entirely different to those of the average man; I did not "go by the book", I had no books, most of the ones I did have had gone down with the boat. The people that I took out boat fishing in Poole Harbour are able to verify these facts. Being "on the spot" had taught me a lot. Here, at the end of my garden, are two salmon; they have shifted a heap of gravel and covered the eggs. These are rare fish even to this day. I had them under observation, watching the cock fish drive away the trout who tried to pinch the eggs to eat. These trout are present, because they are fed with waste scraps from the table. A neighbour's little boy came down to the river to see the fish once, and his mother came after him.

I asked, 'Can he swim?'

She answered, 'No, he can't and he's not going into the water until he can.'

Beware of the Bull

I am now going to tell a fishy story, some of which you may not believe; however, a small bit of fiction has been woven into it, to sort of bind it together.

Soon after I came to Wherwell, I took a small share in a local syndicate, which rented a mile of trout fishing on a nearby little stream. There were only four other members and these all wore funny round hats decorated with numerous flies – I was the odd man out, refraining from this purist folly. Perhaps by joining this "busmen's holiday" you may think I was mad, but, you see, I was not permitted to fish the water that I had charge of – it's not done on the Test – so for the want of some sport, I paid the fee, £50, also some more money to net out coarse fish and restock with 200 trout. As I said, it cost a bit, more than we could really afford, so it was decided to find one or two more members to share in the expense. Thus, it was entrusted to me to lure at least one fellow into our party, so I had a good excuse for spending some evenings in the local, this being a likely place to meet my man.

The Anchor is Let Go

After three weeks, I had failed to gain the confidence of anyone in our district, so I started frequenting an inn a few miles away. Four more wasted evenings went by and then on the fifth night, thinking about how much all my pints had cost me, a well-to-do and smartly dressed gent walked in. It wasn't long before we began to get on speaking terms and I was soon telling him about the joys of trout fishing, and I was also describing our own bit of water, adding that it was possible to forget about the garden and income tax. He seemed to be becoming really interested, so I told him that I had a complete outfit of slightly used tackle, which would be cheap at £70. Then I added that the rent was a mere £50, plus another £45 for restocking and incidentals.

At this stage, he began to fidget and emptied his glass, so I hastily called for two more, I must try to win him over at all costs. Then I told him he could pay by instalments; also, that I would teach him to cast for only one guinea an hour, my usual charge being two guineas (of course, at the same time, it would be good practice for me).

Explaining that my cousin was an agent for a firm of fly-tiers, I told him about the sizes and numbers of the many sorts of winged insects, that there were only 300 different ones, and six sizes of each (2,100 in all); these could be purchased by degrees at 5 per cent below cost price.

He now began to look ill; I don't know what had come over him, so I fetched two more drinks. I then started to talk in a more cautious manner, saying that if he preferred, I had a complete fly-tier's outfit for only £25. Also, I had some fisherman's clothes for only £8 and I would throw in some funny little hats.

He half rose from his chair, so I pushed him back and at the same time, called for two large brandies. Perhaps, after all, I would give him the old clothes; these had accumulated since the Welfare State had abolished tramps and beggars. Besides, my wife had threatened to burn them in any case, so possibly this very generous gesture of mine might win him over. I then started to tell him all about the huge trout in our waters, getting up on my feet, so that I could fully extend my arms. In doing so, I knocked over all our glasses, had to get refills and had to pay for the damage; after this diversion, my intended victim was inclined to ask a few questions. What had we done with the coarse fish we had netted out?

I told him we had 2,250 roach, 4,500 dace and hundreds of grayling and they had all gone to a club's lake in Wiltshire. He suggested it might be more economical to join that club. Then he went on talking about a fly called "Dynamite" and that he had just seen the light of day, although it was nearly 10.00 p.m. I pretended to ignore these remarks as I wriggled in my seat, for it came to mind how the whole camp had fish for supper one evening during the First World War.

A strange feeling came into my mind; this man was to slip my net, all my talk had failed to land him, there was something about him I could not fathom, and I was to be rudely snubbed and humiliated.

He looked me straight in the face and, in a few words, knocked the bottom out of my world.

'I am a very busy man, I happen to be the medical officer at the County Mental Hospital,' he said.

Lost for words, I muttered, 'You have almost a full house, so I have been told.'

'Yes, that is correct, but we might have room for just one more.' It was me who was now feeling very queer. He continued, 'Must see my brother, the rent he is charging you is not nearly enough for such a wonderful length of water. My brother happens to be the riparian owner of this fishery – you might care to know.'

Just at that moment, the barman called "Time", so I slipped out into the cold, dark night, almost a nervous wreck. It took me several days before I became my usual cocky self and felt fit enough to talk the matter over with my other angling partners. Finally, we decided to give up our trout-fishing water and join the club who owned the lake to which our coarse fish had gone. Here, we would only have to pay two guineas each to fish for the whole season. To think that we had caught all those fish earlier with nets, and now we would catch them again, but with hooks this time. What did it matter if we did have to pay to catch what had been our fish once? Besides, they would have become very much larger by this time.

So it came about that we read various articles, all telling us how easy it is to catch huge quantities of very large coarse fish – the fish in the lake must have become monsters by now. All fish add weight, according to tales that are told, especially those that got away.

For our first visit, we phoned the inn, which was only a field away from the lake, booking bed and breakfast for Friday and Saturday night. We spent the first evening in the bar, trying to learn something from the natives. After a while, they told us where to get off as they scratched their heads and nudged each other with their elbows, but we already knew beforehand where to get off – but that's beside the point – I had bought a timetable of the buses which stop at the inn.

> It is called "THE BULL" and the host
> Is a Mr Bill Ware
> Over the door it says: "B. WARE. THE BULL"
> Across the road, in the field, it says:
> "BEWARE OF THE BULL"
> So far, we have not ventured beyond the inn.

38

Reflections

One is much safer at sea than on the land, especially since the great increase of motor traffic on our roads. I travelled 38,000 miles on the open sea in my little boat, mostly during winter months, yet never managed to drown. Nor did I ever capsize in deep water, only once in shallow water and then Tam righted herself. Always carry two balers, tied to your boat, with a yard of loose string, otherwise they will sink to the bottom before the boat can right itself; she will then be full of water and you will still have a baler to use. If all small craft were built to right themselves in the event of capsizing, there would be far fewer people drowning. Lifeboats have to be of the self-righting type; also, being double-enders, they behave much better in heavy seas.

What happened to Tam, you may ask? Well, when we had to give up our spell on *Thalassa*, I took her to the Stour and used her on most days during those seven years on the river and then, when we went to a smaller river farther inland, I had to sell her. That was a sad day, but two anglers from Poole bought her and she went back to the harbour. Yes, I hated having to sell her, she had been invaluable to me for so many years, she had served my every purpose, she had never let me down, and now, after more than forty years, she is still afloat. In Tam, I had been safer in the English Channel at midnight during a gale than I would have been in Bournemouth Square at midday, or any time of day for that matter.

One incident comes to mind when I had gone on an extra-long trip to fish just south of the Needles; by the afternoon, a gale had built up and I was thinking of setting off for home, when four destroyers suddenly appeared as if from nowhere and they began going round in circles. Soon, they began dropping depth charges.

This went on for ten or fifteen minutes and they were going at such a speed that the waves were breaking right over them. I sat watching the scene, a quarter mile to the south-west. You could tell that the seas were heavy, because when they were in the trough of the waves I could not see the destroyers at all.

Then a dull thud was heard; not much noise, but everything in my boat shook violently. A few moments later, I saw the stern end of a submarine rise almost perpendicularly into the air, before it sank beneath the waves. At the same time, a destroyer had lowered a boat, which was immediately swamped by the seas. A second boat was luckier and I saw about eight survivors picked up, may have been more; my eyes were full of spray, so I could not be certain. It seems that one of the depth charges had found its target and the submarine had blown up as a result – that must have been the thud which shook Tam. The sub appeared to be painted green, but as I've already said, I could not see too well. Three of the destroyers made off into the Solent, one remained, possibly in case there were any more survivors. I set my storm sail and had a very rough journey back. Later on, I heard that on that particular day, one Friday in October 1939, the navy had the most successful day they'd ever had throughout the war in sinking U-boats, two small ones in the English Channel and two larger ones elsewhere.

Reflecting back on a good many years, I think of the old timers – the four-masted sailing ships. On several occasions, I happened to see one under full sail, homeward-bound from Australia, with a cargo of grain; a sight never forgotten; a sight I shall never see again.

As you may have already realised, I have always been fond of ships, yes, attracted to anything that floats, be it big or small, battleship or sampan.

Soon afterwards, we moved to Bournemouth – must have been about 1910 or a bit later – plasticine was on sale, which was not unlike clay and you could mould it into all sorts of things. As a boy, this had a great attraction to me and I bought lots of the stuff, grey in colour, and began making model warships with it. Gradually, I accumulated about 270 ships of every variety, from battleships to tiny torpedo boats. In length, they were anything from seven inches down to 2 inches and I would sometimes assemble the entire fleet on our large dining-room table for manoeuvres. Later on, I obtained more plasticine in various colours and with this, I was able to make models of all our liners, using needles as masts and running cotton through the needle eyes to the fore and aft ends of each ship. I was so keen on shipping that I got to know the tonnage, colour and all the details of all the larger vessels under our flag, and their ports of call. After a few years, I sold the lot for about £4. Fishing and going afloat became uppermost in my mind and took most of my time up.

I can remember going to St Alban's Road once, think it was 31 July, not sure if it was 1912 or 1914. Anyhow, the world's biggest assembly of warships was to take place at Spithead about 2 August and, according to my estimation, a large number of ships would be passing along the Dorset coast. It was a wonderful summer's day – like those we usually got in days long gone by, as I sat on that headland, 400 feet above the sea, with my binoculars.

I didn't have long to wait, as soon, one squadron after another passed, sailing eastwards. There were eight squadrons of battleships and sixty-four ships, followed by two battlecruiser squadrons, four ships in each of them. Here, there and everywhere were hundreds of armoured cruisers, destroyers, torpedo boats and depot ships. Something like 450 naval ships passed that day, to assemble for the greatest review the world has ever known. There were a total of over 600 warships and I was to see those ships again two days later.

What a vast assembly of ships lay at anchor at Spithead, six lines of them, each stretching out for seven miles. Paddle steamers, crammed with spectators, came from all the resorts on the south coast. Every paddler was pressed into service, some little better than tugs, which were only capable of six or seven knots, but they managed to crawl up to Spithead from as far away as Weymouth and Lyme Regis, getting back at around midnight. The faster and larger paddle steamers were able to make two trips each day from resorts within a forty-mile radius, making a normal day trip and then going back again in the evening to see the fleet lit up and the searchlight display.

I went three times in all and enjoyed cruising through the long lines of grey ships. There were ships everywhere, ships and more ships, paddlers, yachts, rowing boats, everything but Noah's Ark. I didn't hear of a single collision, but, back in those days, no one was in a hurry, and nor were any of the forty-two paddlers that cruised through the long lines of anchored ships; we had time to see what we had come for.

In those young days, I had a season ticket on the local steamers. I could go as far west as Torquay or east to Brighton. I would take my rod to many of the resorts and fish. My starting off place was Bournemouth Pier and perhaps my favourite trip was to Southampton to see the great liners. Another nice run was to Weymouth, viewing some of Dorset's magnificent coastal scenery on the way – you don't see this when stood on the cliff tops, you've got to be on the water to appreciate it all.

I must have been born lucky, spending my years by rivers, on Studland Heath, living aboard vessels and sailing our coasts, away from town and city.

39

Hove To

As you already know, during those years spent at Goathorn, I paid a weekly rent of one shilling and sixpence; after that, my harbour dues for *Thalassa* were £4 per year. Then, for the past twenty-five years at the rivers, I paid no rent at all, free accommodation being provided when I went to the Stour, and at the old mill at Dinton, also in the castle by the Avon and finally in a house at Wherwell. For all those years I never paid rates; the very idea, why should a simpleton like me, who lived a simple life, have to pay to have my dustbin emptied when I had to do it myself? I never had any street lighting, and why should I pay for roads on which people drive along in tin boxes and kill themselves, when I didn't even own a car?

In 1965, I had to give up the free house, having retired. By the river, yes, by the river, I had to find a cottage where my wife and I could settle down. The only snag? The rent and rates combined amounted to the huge sum of twenty-five shillings per week; quite a shock when we first began paying this money, but we've sort of got used to it now. Perhaps if I could go back to Goathorn, my wife and I could find somewhere to live together, but all our old cottages had been used as targets in preparation for D-Day, so now they are but a heap of rubble. I met one of the chaps who had helped on this mission when in the army; his chief moan was that he could not find a house to live in.

Because I was always on to the rivers, I saw very little of Poole and the harbour, although I still enjoyed odd days sea fishing between Bournemouth and Southsea, and across on the Isle of Wight. But recently I paid a visit to Poole Quay. Here, I met a number of old fishermen and pilots, some of whom I had not seen for as long as twenty-seven years, but we recognised each other, despite the lapse of time and growing older. I also met Charlie Brown, whom I'd spent many an hour with from as long ago as 1925, when he was a boatman to one of the groups of local pilots. We must have been shaking hands for at least ten minutes, when he said, 'There's my brother, "Jo-Jo" Brown across the road.' Although many yards away, his brother dashed across and began shaking my hand as if he was never going to let go.

Jo-Jo was due to take the *Cranborne* out. She was laden and waiting to sail from Hamburg, the captain waiting patiently on the bridge, but still the handshaking continued and *Cranborne* remained tied up. They should have set sail at two o'clock and it was now long past that hour. Yet still the captain paced the bridge, still the chatter went on, and it was not until 2.50 p.m. that Jo-Jo finally went aboard. Then Charlie, in the belated confusion, slipped the stern ropes first, causing the ship to swing right round with the incoming tide rushing between the quay and the ship's stern. It took another fifteen minutes to bring the bow round to the tide. Jo-Jo had been a local pilot for forty years. I had known him when he had first started and now, at last, he has retired.

I also met young Harvey – what did I say, young? He was now seventy-two. I had known him since we were boys. There was more and more of the old handshaking, and then other old salts came along, more yarns were told and hour after hour passed by. We talked about the ships of sail and tall masts, about the steam yachts, Marconi's, Lady Houston's 2,000 ton *Liberty*, renamed the *Gustavburg*, which often arrived with a load of timber and sailed away with 2,200 tons of clay. And of the old *Suffolk Coast*. too – a mystery ship, which survived the First World War and returned to Poole to resume service for Coast Lines. We also recalled the U-boat that came into the harbour in early 1940, but could find nothing to torpedo, not even Tam, which was astern of *Thalassa* at the time. I learned that many old friends had gone on their Last Voyage and there were moments of sadness as we reflected on them; also, of the changes that had come about over the years.

The quayside was littered with cars; in them, the owners gazed out over the harbour, most of 'em could neither walk nor sail a boat. Then there were the silly questions they asked and the silly answers they got back for asking the said silly questions. Hundreds of motor boats and small yachts lay at their moorings, hardly ever used. Their cotton sails would rip to pieces in half a gale and the tapering masts would snap like matchsticks. Top-heavy cabin cruisers with no lines or stability lay rolling to a force two breeze – nearly made me seasick just to think about it. But I've had my day, if this generation gets any fun out of going afloat, then good luck to 'em.

I looked across to Brownsea Island and beyond it lay Goathorn and the great heath, still farther were the Purbeck Hills, rising to 700 feet. Green and Furzey Islands lay to the west and away across the Wareham Channel, I could see Long and Round Islands. All looked much as it did many years back. Modern Man had failed to find this wild paradise, as the four small islands were fringed with mudbanks and rice grass, so were not easy to approach. Taking a last look round, I managed to get away from the quay just after 6 p.m., later travelling back to Wherwell.

We had some awful weather here in April 1966; seven inches of snow on the 14 April, and heavy storms most other days. The rivers were running very high for that time of year. We stayed indoors a lot, looking at some old picture cards. We found one dating back to 1912, showing the *Bournemouth Queen* alongside the pier, about to sail; I was aboard that very day.

There was one regular passenger who comes to mind; we called him "Algy", but as to why I can't remember – perhaps it was because he was a peculiar kind of fellow; proper Algy, if you see what I mean. He never did any work and yet always had plenty of money and wore the best clothes – and trilby hats. From the start of the season and right up to when the war started in August 1914, Algy never missed a trip; he would be almost the first person aboard, so that he could place his deckchair in the recess abaft the starboard paddle box. Often, I was on this very steamer and said to Algy on one occasion, 'You seem to be one of the fixtures, being usually first on and last off.'

He remarked that he had a weak chest and his doctor had suggested that the sea air might do him some good. As we went on chatting, a gust of wind blew his trilby into the sea.

I blurted out, 'Why, I saw you lose one last week on that rough day going to Ventnor.'

'Yes, I know,' he replied casually, 'I've lost twenty-seven or twenty-eight of them since the middle of last season.'

I was much puzzled the very next day when Algy was back on board with a brand-new trilby, knowing that the shops were shut when he had landed the night before and also that they had not yet opened that very morning. Being curious, and with apologies to the old song, I went up to him and asked, 'Where did you get that hat?'

He replied in a most offhand manner, 'Oh, I keep a few dozen just in case, one never knows, does one?'

I went below for a badly needed tonic and upon returning to the upper deck, I gazed astern. Bobbing on our white wake was a brand-new trilby. Yes, you do meet some queer people during a lifetime.

I have mentioned Algy here to add a lighter note to the end of my story. Muggy is again back in Australia and I have no doubt he will return again. He is sure to come and see me. I dare not tell him about the trout in the river by my garden, as it was in a garden by the river that I first learned to poach; he might have the same idea.